American Language Hub

LEVEL 3B
Student's Book

JEREMY DAY
GARETH REES

macmillan education

Contents

	LESSON • OBJECTIVES	GRAMMAR	VOCABULARY	PRONUNCIATION
U6	SPORTS AND HOBBIES			
6.1	**Take part!** (p62) Describe a sport or game Give a short, persuasive talk	**modals of obligation**	adjectives ending in *–ive* sports	rhythm: pausing
6.2	**Hobbies** (p66) Talk about hobbies and free time activities Discuss trying new things	**present perfect progressive** ***had to / needed to***	hobbies and free time activities	*been*: unstressed
6.3	Café Hub **You got served** (p70) Express your opinion		express an opinion	intonation for expressing opinions
	UNIT REVIEW (p72)	WRITING (pXXIV) Write an article for a magazine | KEY SKILL Introductory clauses		
U7	FOOD			
7.1	**Eating out** (p74) Talk about eating out Make speculations and deductions about food	**modals of speculation and deduction**	phrasal verbs adjectives to describe food	diphthongs word stress with modals
7.2	**Food fads** (p78) Compare different types of food Compare a range of solutions and choose the best one	**comparatives and superlatives** ***the ..., the ...***	waste	vowel + *w*
7.3	Café Hub **Comfort eating** (p82) Make suggestions		making suggestions	suggestions
	UNIT REVIEW (p84)	WRITING (pXXV) Write a reply in an online discussion forum | KEY SKILL Comparing and recommending		
U8	INNOVATION			
8.1	**Making a difference** (p86) Explain how an invention works Suggest and evaluate creative ideas	**adjective clauses**	word families creative thinking	adjective clauses
8.2	**Must-have gadgets** (p90) Use positive language to promote a new product Give a friend advice about choosing a gadget	**zero and first conditionals** **conditionals with modals and imperatives**	positive adjectives	*'ll* and *won't*
8.3	Café Hub **Flat-packed** (p94) Give and follow instructions		giving and following instructions	sentence stress
	UNIT REVIEW (p96)	WRITING (pXXVI) Write a biography | KEY SKILL Using linking words to show contrast		
U9	THE ARTS			
9.1	**Art for everybody** (p98) Suggest improvements to a proposal Plan an art event	**second conditional**	the arts verbal idioms	**/tʃ/**, **/ʃ/** and **/k/**
9.2	**Tell me a story** (p102) Report a conversation Create a collaborative story	**reported speech**	reporting verbs	using your voice to make a story more interesting
9.3	Café Hub **Leaving London** (p106) Talk about movies and books		phrases to talk about movies	words connected to movies
	UNIT REVIEW (p108)	WRITING (pXXVII) Write a review | KEY SKILL Using colons to introduce explanations		
U10	PSYCHOLOGY			
10.1	**Making up your mind** (p110) Talk about different versions of past events Talk about past mistakes	**third conditional** ***should have*** **+ past participle**	psychology verbs expressions with *mind*	third conditional
10.2	**Wish lists** (p114) Talk about your wishes and regrets Plan a to-do list	**hopes and wishes**	reflexive verbs staying organized	emphasis and reflexive pronouns
10.3	Café Hub **Come home** (p118) Make and accept apologies		make and accept apologies	vowel sounds
	UNIT REVIEW (p120)	WRITING (pXXVIII) Write a report | KEY SKILL Writing a report		

READING • LISTENING	SPEAKING • WRITING
read an article about the sport of snowball fighting in Scotland listen to a talk about eSports **KEY SKILL** Listening for main and supporting points	describe a sport or a game and discuss sports **SPEAKING HUB** give a persuasive talk about a sport or a game
listen to a radio show about hobbies and free time activities read about a person who tries something new every month for six months **KEY SKILL** Identifying tone	**SPEAKING HUB** interview your classmates about their free time activities **SPEAKING HUB** talk and ask about new activities
watch a video about different types of food	give an opinion about exercising
read an article about supper clubs **KEY SKILL** Hidden contrasts listen to a conversation at a dinner party	plan and present a supper club **SPEAKING HUB** describe a dish you would like to bring to a dinner party
read a food fad blog listen to a radio show about household food waste **KEY SKILL** Identifying people's opinions	ask and answer questions using superlatives **SPEAKING HUB** give a presentation about how to reduce food waste in the home
watch a video about a problem and a suggestion	talk about possible solutions to problems
read a text about a Canadian inventor read a short text on 'thinking outside the box' listen to friends discussing what you can do to be more creative **KEY SKILL** Listening for problems and solutions	talk about a person, a place and an object **SPEAKING HUB** talk about ideas for creating a website
listen to a podcast about new gadgets read a magazine article about gadgets **KEY SKILL** Topic sentences	invent a new gadget and promote it **SPEAKING HUB** give advice to a friend who wants to buy a gadget
watch a video about people assembling furniture	follow and give practical instructions
listen to finalists from a public art competition read an article about immersive theater **KEY SKILL** Using linking words to understand the writer's opinion	discuss proposals for an art venue and suggest improvements **SPEAKING HUB** discuss ideas for an immersive theater performance
listen to two friends talking about *The Great Gatsby* read an extract from *The Great Gatsby* listen to two friends talking about storytelling **KEY SKILL** Listening for definitions of new words	talk about books and stories and report a conversation **SPEAKING HUB** create and tell a collaborative story
watch a video about a movie	describe a favorite movie
read an article about thinking rationally and decision making listen to a conversation between two friends about a failed shopping trip **KEY SKILL** Listening for phrases that support an argument	discuss different outcomes of past events **SPEAKING HUB** discuss past mistakes
listen to a conversation on the power of habit read about the psychology of the to-do list **KEY SKILL** Bridge sentences	talk about wishes, hopes, regrets and dreams **SPEAKING HUB** make a wish list into a to-do list
watch a video about an apology	act out conversations to make and accept apologies

Irregular verbs (pIV) **Grammar Hub** (pVI) **Vocabulary Hub** (pXVI) **Communication Hub** (pXIX) **Audio scripts** (pXXIX)

Irregular Verbs

Base form	Simple past	Past participle
be	was/were	been
become	became	become
begin	began	begun
break	broke	broken
bring	brought	brought
build	built	built
buy	bought	bought
can	could	been able to
catch	caught	caught
choose	chose	chosen
come	came	come
cost	cost	cost
cut	cut	cut
drink	drank	drunk
eat	ate	eaten
fall	fell	fallen
feel	felt	felt
find	found	found
forget	forgot	forgotten
get	got	got
give	gave	given
go	went	gone/been
grow	grew	grown
have	had	had
hear	heard	heard
hit	hit	hit
hold	held	held
hurt	hurt	hurt
keep	kept	kept
know	knew	known
leave	left	left
lend	lent	lent
let	let	let

Base form	Simple past	Past participle
lose	lost	lost
make	made	made
mean	meant	meant
meet	met	met
must	had to	had to
pay	paid	paid
put	put	put
read	read	read
ride	rode	ridden
run	ran	run
say	said	said
see	saw	seen
sell	sold	sold
send	sent	sent
set	set	set
shut	shut	shut
sing	sang	sung
sit	sat	sat
sleep	slept	slept
speak	spoke	spoken
spell	spelled	spelled
spend	spent	spent
stand	stood	stood
steal	stole	stolen
take	took	taken
teach	taught	taught
tell	told	told
think	thought	thought
throw	threw	thrown
understand	understood	understood
wear	wore	worn
win	won	won
write	wrote	written

PHONETIC SYMBOLS											
Single vowels			Diphthongs			Consonants					
/ɪ/	fish	/fɪʃ/	/uw/	news	/nuw/	/p/	pen	/pen/	/s/	snake	/sneɪk/
/iː/	bean	/biːn/	/eɪ/	face	/feɪs/	/b/	bag	/bæg/	/z/	zoo	/zuː/
/ʊ/	foot	/fʊt/	/ɔɪ/	boy	/bɔɪ/	/t/	tea	/tiː/	/ʃ/	shop	/ʃɒp/
/uː/	shoe	/ʃuː/	/oʊ/	nose	/noʊz/	/d/	dog	/dɒg/	/ʒ/	television	/ˈtelɪvɪʒən/
/e/	egg	/eg/	/ju/	use	/juz/	/ʧ/	chip	/ʧɪp/	/m/	map	/mæp/
/ə/	mother	/ˈmʌðər/	/aɪ/	eye	/aɪ/	/ʤ/	jazz	/ʤæz/	/n/	name	/neɪm/
/ɜː/	word	/wɜːrd/	/aʊ/	mouth	/maʊθ/	/k/	cake	/keɪk/	/ŋ/	ring	/rɪŋ/
/ɔː/	talk	/tɔːk/				/g/	girl	/gɜːrl/	/h/	house	/haʊs/
/æ/	back	/bæk/				/f/	film	/fɪlm/	/l/	leg	/leg/
/ʌ/	bus	/bʌs/				/v/	verb	/vɜːrb/	/r/	road	/roʊd/
/ɑː/	arm	/ɑːrm/				/θ/	thing	/θɪŋ/	/w/	want	/wɒnt/
/ɒ/	top	/tɒp/				/ð/	these	/ðiːz/	/j/	yes	/jes/

6 SPORTS AND HOBBIES

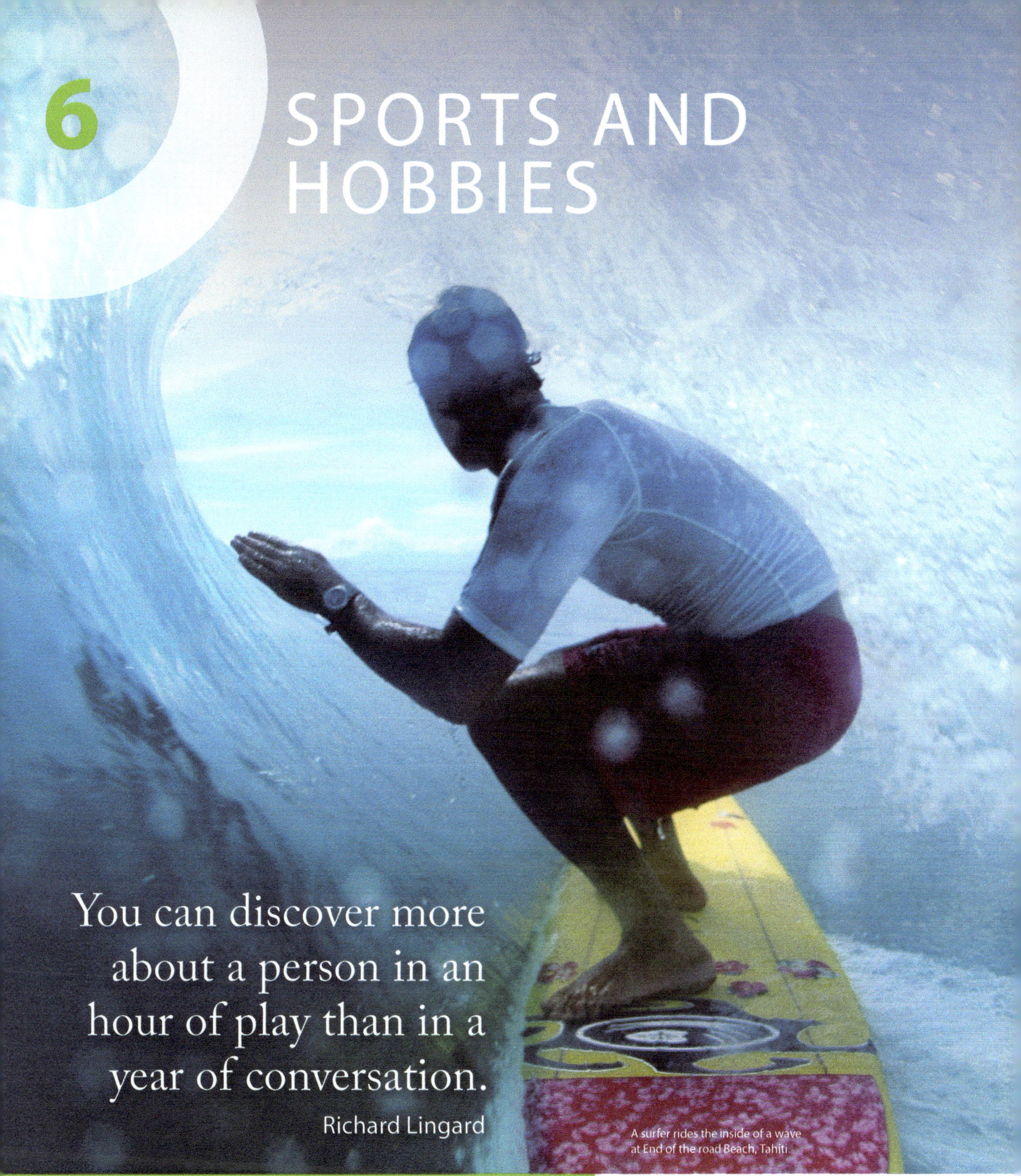

A surfer rides the inside of a wave at End of the road Beach, Tahiti.

> You can discover more about a person in an hour of play than in a year of conversation.
>
> Richard Lingard

- describe a sport or game
- give a short, persuasive talk
- talk about hobbies and free time activities
- discuss trying new things
- express your opinion
- write an article for a magazine

Work with a partner. Discuss the questions.

1 Do you agree with the quote?

2 Look at the picture. Why do some people take part in sports like this?

3 How interested are you in these free time activities?

team sports · running · music · collecting

6.1 Take part!

- Describe a sport or game
- Give a short, persuasive talk

G modals of obligation V adjectives ending in *-ive;* sports P rhythm: pausing
S listening for main and supporting points

COMPETITIVE SNOWBALL FIGHTING HITS SCOTLAND!

If you think snowball fights are just for school kids, think again. **Competitive** snowball fighting (*Yukigassen*) is a sport for grown-ups that has just arrived in Scotland.

It began as an official sport in Japan in 1987 and since then it has spread to countries such as Canada, Australia, Norway and Sweden. And this weekend sees the first ever matches in Scotland.

Angus Campbell, the captain of the Glasgow Ice Warriors, says 'I think *Yukigassen* is going to be **massive** here. We have the snow and it's a fun and **inexpensive** sport that's **attractive** to everyone. Each match only lasts nine minutes, so you don't have to be super athletic to take part in a game.'

The snowball fights take place on a small court (40 m x 10 m) between two teams of seven players – each team must include male and female members. To win a game, a team has to capture the other team's flag or take out all their opponents with direct snowball hits. If a player is hit, he or she has to leave the game.

The rules are fairly simple, but Angus insists that having an **effective** strategy is the key to success. 'You must work together as a team, be **decisive** and keep calm when under pressure from your opponents. You shouldn't just run for the flag – you'll soon get hit and be out. You need to be more **creative** than that. Your team only has 90 snowballs, which the referee gives you before the game. You must not make any more during the game.'

Six teams are taking part in the event this weekend, and there will be trial sessions for anyone who wants to try it out. 'It looks a little **aggressive** at first, but you shouldn't feel nervous. It's only snow, and all players have to wear a helmet, which we'll provide. However, you should bring some warm gloves!'

If you're interested in trying something **active** on these cold winter days, you simply must go. The games are **impressive** to watch, and great to play. After all, what's more fun than playing in the snow?

The first game starts at 2 pm, on Saturday, in the city park. Entrance is free. Families are welcome.

READING

A SPEAK Write down the names of the different sports you know in pictures 1–4. Then check with another student. What do you know about these sports? Tell your partner.

B READ FOR GIST Read *Competitive snowball fighting hits Scotland!* Where do you think the article comes from? Why?

- a a national newspaper
- b a sports science academic journal
- c a local news and information website
- d a travel blog

C READ FOR DETAIL Put the sentences in the order the information appears in the article.

- a New players do not need to bring any safety equipment. ___
- b There are two ways to beat the other team. ___
- c There are men and women on every team. ___
- d Generally, people think children, not adults, have snowball fights. 1
- e A good game plan is important. ___
- f Several countries play competitive snowball fighting. ___

D SPEAK Work in pairs. What is your opinion of *Yukigassen*? Would you like to play it?

GRAMMAR
Modals of obligation

A WORK IT OUT Look at the sentences from *Competitive snowball fighting hits Scotland!* Write *nc* (you have no choice, this is 100 percent necessary) or *c* (you have a choice, this is not necessary) next to each sentence.

1 All players **have to** wear a protective helmet. ___
2 You **don't have to** be super athletic. ___
3 You **should** bring some warm gloves. ___
4 You **shouldn't** just run for the flag. ___
5 Each team **must** include male and female members. ___
6 You **must not** make any more during the game. ___
7 You **shouldn't** feel nervous. ___

B Match the beginnings of the rules (1–4) with the endings (a–d).

Modals of obligation	
1 We use *must* / *have to* / *need to*	a to talk about what is or is not a good idea.
2 We use *must not* when	b for rules and situations that are necessary (strong obligation).
3 We use *don't have to* when	c we describe things that are not necessary, but you may still do them.
4 We use *should* / *shouldn't*	d we describe something that is not allowed.

C Go to the Grammar Hub on page VI.

D SPEAK Work in pairs. Compare the pairs of sports below. How are they similar and different? Think about their basic rules and the qualities of good players and successful teams.

baseball and cricket   soccer and basketball
marathon running and running a 100 meter race   tennis and racquetball

VOCABULARY
Adjectives ending in *-ive*

A Look at the adjectives in bold in *Competitive snowball fighting hits Scotland!* Then complete the definitions with the correct adjective.

1 A ______________ person makes choices quickly and confidently.
2 A ______________ sport involves two teams trying to beat each other.
3 If something is ______________, it is very big or, in informal English, very popular.
4 An ______________ suggestion or idea is one that people are interested in.
5 An ______________ plan works well and produces the result that is wanted.
6 An ______________ activity doesn't cost a lot of money to do.
7 Having an ______________ lifestyle means you do not sit around all day.
8 ______________ behavior includes being rude or angry in order to get what you want.
9 You admire an ______________ performance because it is very good and shows a lot of skill.
10 A ______________ person thinks of new or unusual ways to do things.

B SPEAK Complete the questions with adjectives from Exercise A. Then work in pairs and interview your partner. Take turns. Give reasons and examples to explain your answers.

1 What is the most ______________ sport that you have played?
2 Are you a very ______________ person? Why do you say that?
3 Which actors do you think are very ______________?

SPEAKING

A You are going to write six sentences to describe a sport or game without naming it. Your classmates will try to guess what it is. Think about:

- reasons why you like it.
- the skills and qualities you need to play it well.
- how it is played and what you need to play it.

B Work in groups. Read your sentences to the group. Can your classmates guess the sport or game?

C Work in groups and discuss the questions.

1 Which of the sports and games described have you played? What do you think of them?
2 Which haven't you played? Would you like to try them?
3 Which is the most popular sport or game?

LISTENING

A SPEAK Work in pairs and discuss the questions. What are the pros and cons of playing video games?

6.1 **B LISTEN FOR GIST** Listen to a talk about eSports and choose the correct answers.

1 What is the best title for the talk?
   a Video gaming: is it good for you?
   b Video gaming: the professional sport of the future
   c Video gaming: nothing more than a free time activity
   d Video gaming: the next Olympic sport?
2 What is the purpose of the talk?
   a to give general information about eSports
   b to encourage people to watch and play eSports
   c to persuade people to agree with the speaker's opinion of eSports
   d to give a balanced analysis of eSports

6.1 **C LISTEN FOR DETAIL** Listen again to the introduction. What is the main idea of the talk? What are the supporting points? Use the strategies in the box to help you.

Listening for main and supporting points

When giving a talk, speakers usually give a main idea and then support it with detailed points, in the form of examples, statistics, names or dates.

Listen carefully to identify the main ideas and the supporting points that follow.

6.2 **D** Listen again to another part of the talk. What is the main idea? What are the supporting points?

6.1 **E LISTEN FOR DETAIL** Listen again to the whole talk and choose the correct answers.

1 The speaker thinks that many people in the audience …
   a play video games at home.
   b understand how popular eSports are.
   c don't realize that video gaming is played professionally.
2 She says playing video games is a sport because …
   a players practice a lot.
   b the games have clear rules.
   c there are winners and losers.
3 She says a great eSports player
   a has a strong mind and body.
   b plays other traditional sports.
   c spends all their time training.
4 She says eSports are different from traditional sports because …
   a they are growing in popularity.
   b young people like them.
   c people watch them online.
5 The Olympic Games wants to include sports that …
   a involve physical activity.
   b young people like.
   c have professional players.

F SPEAK Work in pairs and discuss the questions.

1 In your opinion, what is the difference between a sport and a game?
2 Do you agree with the speaker's arguments? Which of her points do you think are strong or weak?
3 Do you think eSports should be an Olympic sport? Why/Why not?

VOCABULARY

Sports

A Check (✓) the nouns that refer to people.

1 champion	☐	6 stadium	☐
2 coach	☐	7 fan	☐
3 final	☐	8 top player	☐
4 league	☐	9 tournament	☐
5 spectator	☐	10 trophy	☐

B Complete the sentences with the correct form of the nouns in Exercise A.

1 In the Olympic Games, the winners receive a gold medal, not a ________________.

2 Usain Bolt and Michael Phelps are two of the most famous Olympic ________________.

3 The FIFA World Cup is a soccer ________________ that is held every four years.

4 If you are a Manchester United ________________, you should wear something red to the game.

5 The Camp Nou, in Barcelona, is the largest soccer ________________ in Europe. It can hold nearly 100,000 ________________.

6 ________________ can earn a lot of money from advertising and sponsorship contracts.

7 If a team loses a lot of games, the ________________ usually loses his or her job.

8 Nothing in sport is certain – you don't always see the two best teams in a ________________.

9 There are 20 teams in the national ________________. Each team plays the others twice, so each team plays 38 games in a year.

C SPEAK **Work in groups and discuss the questions.**

1 What are the popular spectator sports and sports tournaments in your country?

2 Who are the top sportsmen and women in your country? What do you know about them?

PRONUNCIATION

Rhythm: pausing

Pausing

We use pauses to support the meaning of what we say, and to help the listener follow and understand.

- Use very short pauses to group words that go together in phrases or clauses. This is similar to using a comma in writing, but can be more frequent.
- Use short pauses at the end of sentences and paragraphs. This is similar to using a period in writing.
- Make the pauses a little longer to add emphasis or drama.

6.3 **A** **Listen to the beginning of the talk about eSports. Mark where the speaker pauses. The first two pauses have been marked (/) to help you. Which pauses are longer to add emphasis or drama?**

Soccer, / basketball, / golf, tennis – four of the world's most popular sports. They are played by millions and watched by millions more, and all four are in the greatest festival of sports, the Olympic Games.

6.4 **B** **Where do you think the speaker pauses in the next part of the talk? Mark (/) each pause. Then listen and check your answer.**

However, there is one sport that is just as popular as those, but it still hasn't been accepted in the Olympics, and indeed, many people say that it is not even a sport. What sport am I talking about? eSports. Yes, electronic sports, or competitive video gaming.

C SPEAK **Work in pairs. Practice saying the extracts in Exercises A and B. Listen and check that your partner pauses in the correct places.**

SPEAKING HUB

A **You are going to give a short persuasive talk (1–3 minutes). Choose one of the titles and write notes for your talk.**

- eSports are not sports and should not be part of the Olympic Games.
- Playing video games is a good activity for children.
- Video games are generally more negative than positive.
- Professional athletes earn too much money. Their pay should be limited.
- ________________ is the best sport to both play and watch.

B PLAN **Look at your notes and use these tips on how to improve a persuasive talk.**

- Have a good introduction and conclusion.
- Use confident language, e.g. *I strongly believe …; It's undoubtedly true that …*
- Use rhetorical questions, e.g. *Why should we do this?; I'm sure you agree, don't you?*
- Support your main points with good examples and arguments.
- Practice your pausing and rhythm when giving the talk.

C PRESENT **Work in groups. Give your talks. Write down the main ideas and supporting points of the other talks.**

D REFLECT **Work in groups. Did you agree or disagree with the speakers? Which points do you think were strongest?**

Describe a sport or game

Give a short, persuasive talk

6.2 Hobbies

- Talk about hobbies and free time activities
- Discuss trying new things

V – hobbies and free time activities
S – identifying tone
G – present perfect progressive; *had to / needed to*
P – *been*: unstressed

LISTENING

A SPEAK **Work in pairs and discuss the questions.**

1 Describe the pictures (a–e). What are the people doing?
2 Which free time activities are you most interested in? Why?

6.5 **B LISTEN FOR GIST** **Listen to a radio show about hobbies and free time activities. Match the pictures (a–e) with the guest speakers (1–5).**

1 ___ 2 ___ 3 ___ 4 ___ 5 ___

6.5 **C LISTEN FOR DETAIL** **Listen again. Choose the best answers for each person.**

1 Speaker 1
  a buys and sells new cars.
  b spends a lot of money on his hobby.
  c makes enough money from his hobby to pay for his vacations.
2 Speaker 2
  a finds his hobby stressful at times.
  b also works as a photographer.
  c is learning how to do something new.
3 Speaker 3
  a wants her husband to spend more time on his hobby.
  b says her husband spends a lot of time on his hobby.
  c shares her husband's hobby.
4 Speaker 4
  a shares her interest with her friends.
  b has her own social media site about her interest.
  c regularly stays at hotels in Boston.
5 Speaker 5
  a usually has a few hobbies at the same time.
  b finds it hard to get interested in things.
  c has had many different hobbies.

D SPEAK **Work in groups and discuss the questions.**

1 Are there any hobbies you would like to try? Which ones?
2 What are the benefits of having a hobby?

VOCABULARY

Hobbies and free time activities

A WORK IT OUT **Look at the three sets of verb phrases from the radio show. Match the beginnings of the phrases with the endings (a–d).**

1	join	a	interest in a hobby
	be	b	a hobby
	lose	c	a society
	take up	d	my thing
2	be	a	into something
	be	b	you in shape
	keep	c	of a singer
	be a fan	d	a member of a fan club
3	get	a	relaxing
	be	b	from daily stress
	collect	c	you out of the house
	escape	d	something, like stamps or art

B **Complete the table with the verb phrases from Exercise A.**

Show enthusiasm for a hobby	Something you may do as part of a hobby	Benefits of a hobby	Start a new hobby
be into something	___	___	___
___	___	___	
___	___	___	
___		___	
___			

C **Go to the Vocabulary Hub on page XVI.**

D SPEAK **Rewrite these sentences so they are true for you. Then work in pairs and compare your answers. Give reasons and examples.**

1 I'm a big fan of the singer Ed Sheeran.
2 I need to find a way to get myself out of the house more frequently.
3 I've collected a lot of different things during my life.
4 I don't do much to stay in shape. I should do more.
5 I've never been a member of a fan club nor joined a society.
6 Cooking isn't really my thing.
7 I've had a few hobbies that I've lost interest in.
8 This year, I've taken up a new hobby.

d

e

GRAMMAR

Present perfect progressive

A WORK IT OUT **Look at the sentences from the radio show and choose the correct answers.**

1 Which sentence describes a single action that continues up to now? Which sentences describe an action or activity that is frequently repeated up to now?

   a He's been doing it since his teens.

   b We've been waiting here all day.

   c For the last six months, I've been going to pottery classes.

2 In each sentence, is the main verb a state or an action verb?

   a He's been doing it since his teens.

   b I've had this interest since I was a child.

   c I've been a member of his fan club for a long time.

3 What are the recently completed actions in the sentences? Which sentence focuses on the fact that the action is completed? Which sentence focuses on the duration of the action?

   a I've been working in the studio this afternoon – that's why my hands are so dirty.

   b I've just bought an old Mini, so I'll start working on that tomorrow.

B **Complete the rules (1–5) with the words in the box.**

progressive	long	now	past	present	repeated	state

Present perfect progressive

1 We usually use the present perfect progressive to talk about an action that started in the ________________ and is continuing ________________. The emphasis is on the unfinished activity.

2 We also use it to talk about a past action that has just finished, but which has a ________________ result.

3 We can use it to talk about ________________ or frequently ________________ actions.

4 We do not use the present perfect progressive with ________________ verbs.

5 We use the present perfect progressive to talk about how ________________ something has been happening.

C Go to the Grammar Hub on page VI.

D SPEAK Work in pairs. Student A – go to the Communication Hub on page XIX. Student B – go to the Communication Hub on page XXIII.

PRONUNCIATION

been: unstressed

6.6 **A** **Listen to three sentences. What do you notice about the pronunciation of *been* in each sentence? Does it rhyme with *seen* or *thin*?**

been

In the present perfect progressive, *been* is an auxiliary verb and it is normally unstressed and pronounced /bɪn/.

The stressed words are usually the main verbs and key information words, not the auxiliary verbs.

6.7 **B** **Listen and repeat.**

SPEAKING HUB

A **Choose one of your hobbies or free time activities and prepare to talk about it. Answer the following questions.**

1 When did you take it up and why?

2 How much time and money do you spend on it?

3 What do you like about it?

4 Is there anything you dislike about it?

5 What benefits does it bring to you and your life?

6 Why would someone else enjoy your hobby?

B SPEAK **Go around the class and interview three or four of your classmates about their hobbies. Write notes.**

C DISCUSS **Work in groups. Tell each other about your interviews. Which hobbies were:**

- the most unusual?
- the most interesting?
- the most dangerous?
- the most expensive?

READING

A SPEAK Work in pairs. When was the last time you:

- tried a new food or drink?
- listened to a new singer or group?
- visited a new place?

B READ FOR MAIN IDEA Read the first two paragraphs of *My six months of trying new things*. Then complete the summary with a word in the box.

interesting relaxing

Candie is not very active. She decided to spend the first six months of this year doing different activities because she wants to find a hobby that will make her free time more ______________.

My six months of trying new things

By Candie Carmichael

July 15

I've never been the kind of person who does lots of exciting things in their free time. Paragliding, swimming with dolphins, climbing Mount Everest – not me! My idea of danger is to sit on the couch and watch the latest crime series on TV. The closest I get to nature is when I 'like' my friends' cat pictures on social media. As for climbing Himalayan mountains – forget it! I'd rather climb the stairs to bed.

But at one point toward the end of last year, I started to feel that my life was becoming a little … well … boring. I needed to take up a hobby. But which one? There are so many things out there – how do you know what you will enjoy? So I decided to spend the first six months of this year trying out a new hobby each month. I was a complete beginner at every activity I tried.

Here's what happened:

January: Fly fishing

The first thing I learned was that no flies are harmed in fly fishing. You make a pretty, artificial 'fly' and attach it to a hook on a fishing line. [1]___ When a fish takes a bite you … oh, I don't know. I did NOT do well at this. One month: lots of badly made 'flies', and ZERO fish (apart from the ones I got at the fish and fries place on my way home).

February: Stamp collecting

Why does anyone do this? [2]___ After a whole four weeks of attaching little squares of paper from around the world into a big book with blank pages, I still have no idea.

March: Ping-Pong

This one really surprised me. I'm actually good at it! I joined a club, and I didn't need to spend a lot of time practicing before I started winning games. After only a month, I was already one of the best players in the group. I really can't believe it. [3]___

April: Beekeeping

Surely all I had to do was keep some flying insects in a box? [4]___ About a hundred bee stings later, I realized that a lot can go wrong and beekeeping is a serious (and sometimes painful) business. I think I'll just get my honey from the grocery store in future.

May: Playing the ukulele

The ukulele is like a very small guitar. It has four strings. It makes you look like a giant when you play it. [5]___ I didn't have to be in great shape. It wasn't dangerous and it wasn't painful. And at the end of the month, I could play *Rivers of Babylon* all the way through. If that isn't success, I don't know what is!

C READ FOR KEY WORDS Read the rest of the article. Match the activities (1–6) with Candie's experiences (a–f).

1 fly fishing
2 stamp collecting
3 yoga
4 beekeeping
5 playing the ukulele
6 Ping-Pong

a This hobby caused her pain.
b She wasn't successful at all.
c She was able to complete a whole song.
d She was surprised by how good she was at this activity.
e She learned that she is not able to do this kind of thing well because she isn't athletic.
f She didn't understand why this is a popular hobby.

D READ FOR DETAIL Read again. Fill in the blanks in the article (1–6) with the sentences (a–f).

a Is this really a hobby?
b What could possibly go wrong?
c Maybe there's a chance for me to get in shape after all.
d Then you throw the line on the water.
e I really enjoyed this.
f I am not very flexible.

Identifying tone

An essay or serious news article will usually have a formal or serious tone. Other kinds of text, like emails between friends or some web or magazine articles, may have an informal or humorous tone.

You can identify a text's tone from the way it is written and the author's choice of phrases, adverbs and adjectives, capital letters and punctuation.

E Look at the highlighted words and phrases. What do the capital letters, punctuation and word choice tell us about the article's tone?

F SPEAK Work in pairs. If you had to choose one of these activities to take up for a month, which would you choose? Why? Tell your partner.

June: Yoga

Ouch! I thought yoga was relaxing. I didn't realize I had to be super athletic and flexible. After one month of downward dogs and (falling over!) tree poses, I learned some very important things about me: I am not very athletic. 6___ I do not like yoga.

GRAMMAR

had to / needed to

A WORK IT OUT Look at the sentences from *My six months of trying new things*. Then choose the correct words to complete the rules.

I needed to take up a hobby.

All I had to do was keep some flying insects in a box.

I didn't have to be in great shape.

I didn't need to spend a lot of time practicing before I started winning games.

had to / needed to

1 We use ***had to*** and ***needed to*** when we talk about things that were necessary in the ***present / past***.

2 We use ***didn't have to*** and ***didn't need to*** when we talk about things that were ***not allowed / not necessary but possible*** in the past.

B Go to the Grammar Hub on page VI.

C SPEAK Work in pairs. Tell your partner:

- three things you *had to / needed to* do yesterday. Explain why.
- three things you *didn't have to / didn't need to* do yesterday. Explain why.

SPEAKING HUB

A Think of one or two new activities that you have tried. Use the list to help you or your own ideas.

get a pet
plant flowers or grow a plant
make a birthday present instead of buying one
try a new form of exercise
take language classes
make a photo album
learn a new board game

B PLAN Think about:

- how and why you did it.
- what was easy/difficult about it.
- the things you had to / needed to do.
- the things you didn't have to / didn't need to do.
- why you stopped/continued doing it.

C SPEAK Work in pairs. Tell your partner about the new activity you tried. Then listen to your partner and ask him/her questions about the activity.

○– Talk about hobbies and free time activities
○– Discuss trying new things

Café Hub

6.3 You got served

F– express your opinion P– intonation for expressing opinions

COMPREHENSION

A Work in pairs. Tell your partner how you prepare for exercising or playing sports. What do you do before you start?

B ▶ 00:00–00:32 Watch the first part of the video. Are any of the things you discussed in Exercise A in the video? Who do you think will win the game?

C ▶ 00:33–03:15 Watch the second part of the video. Check (✓) *Gaby* or *Sam* or both.

Gaby	Sam	
		thinks it's unusual to put butter on toast.
		thinks British breakfast is more than buttered toast and milky tea.
		thinks Spanish food is better than English food.
		thinks tortilla is boring.
		changes their mind at the end.

FUNCTIONAL LANGUAGE

Expressing your opinion

A ▶ Complete the phrases in the table. Then watch the video again and check your answers.

Give an opinion	I [1]________ that's very strange. [2]________ you think that's horrible? I [3]________ British food is better than ever these days. In my [4]________, British food is still really bad. If you ask [5]________, it's your opinion that's really bad. Spanish food is so much better. Don't [6]________ agree? Do you know [7]________ I think? Tortilla is a bit boring.
Give examples to support an opinion	[8]________ instance, … To give you an example, …
Agree with an opinion	I agree. You are probably [9]________. Absolutely!
Disagree with an opinion	I disagree. I [10]________ don't think that's true. Nonsense. To be brutally [11]________, no!

B Work in groups. Decide which are the three countries with the best food in the world.

MILLY SAM NEENA ZAC GABY

USEFUL PHRASES

A Match the useful phrases (1–5) with the phrases that come before or after them (a–e). Then watch the video and check your answers.

1 Game, set and match – Sam!
2 Not hugely.
3 Wake up! Say something!
4 I didn't realize you were so passionate about food.
5 British food is average!

a So you don't like Spanish food?
b Sam, are you OK?
c I'm sorry! I got a bit angry.
d I was right!
e Nonsense!

B How do you say these useful phrases in your language?

PRONUNCIATION

Intonation for expressing opinions

6.8 **A** Listen and repeat the extracts from the video. Copy the stress and intonation.

A: In my opinion, British food is still really bad.
B: Well, if you ask me, it's your opinion that's really bad.
A: Spanish food is so much better – don't you agree?
B: To be brutally honest, no!
A: Do you want to know what I think? I think tortilla is a bit boring.
B: Boring!

B Work in pairs. Make similar conversations. Change the information.

SPEAKING

A Complete the statements with opinion phrases from Functional Language Exercise A.

... eat before exercising.

If you ask me, you shouldn't eat for one hour before exercising.

... do an hour of aerobic exercise every day.

___

... tennis is more exciting to watch than soccer.

___

... the gym is boring.

___

... female athletes should be paid the same as men.

___

... running is the best sport in the world.

___

... boxing is too violent.

___

... eSports are more exciting than real sports.

___

B DISCUSS Work in pairs. Take turns reading out your statements from Exercise A and agree or disagree with your partner's statements.

Express your opinion

➤ Turn to page XXIV to learn how to write an article for a magazine.

Unit 6 Review

GRAMMAR

A Complete the conversation between a soccer coach and some new players with the correct modals of obligation.

Coach: The rules say so. You [1] ______________ touch the ball with your hands. It isn't allowed.

Player 1: But what about the goalkeeper? He sometimes [2] ______________ use his hand to stop a shot. I've seen it on TV.

Coach: OK, OK! Everyone except the goalkeeper [3] ______________ follow that rule. And you all [4] ______________ warm up before a game. I insist on that. If you don't warm up, you don't play.

Player 2: I can't get here until 6 pm.

Coach: That's a little late, the game starts at 6:15 pm. You [5] ______________ start warming up at 5:45, by 6 pm at the latest. You bike here, don't you? If so, you [6] ______________ do a big warm-up. But you [7] ______________ be here by six, OK?

B Complete the TV interview with the present perfect or present progressive form of the verbs in parentheses.

Reporter: Hi, everyone. I'm with champion surfer Sally Gowen. Sally, [1] ____________ you ____________ (*surf*) here all day?

Surfer: Hi, Maisie. Yes, I sure have. The water [2] ______________________ (*be*) excellent all day. I love it here. I [3] ______________________ (*come*) here a lot recently.

Reporter: What [4] ______________ you ______________ (*practice*) today? Some new moves?

Surfer: No, no. Nothing too special. OK, I'm going back on the surf now.

Reporter: Oh, I [5] ______________________ (*finish*) yet. Just one more … Sally? Sally! Oh, she [6] ______________________ (*go*).

C Complete the text with *had to*, *didn't have to*, *needed to* or *didn't need to*. Sometimes more than one answer is possible.

I remember my first year at college well. It was so different from being at high school. Finally, we [1] ______________ wear a uniform every day, and I [2] ______________ tell my parents where I was all the time. I enjoyed that new freedom, and I [3] ______________ grow up quickly, too. I [4] ______________ take more responsibility for everyday things. I was lucky though because I lived in a student residence. I [5] ______________ live there, but I chose to because I wanted to meet other people easily. It was a good decision. We [6] ______________ follow a few rules, but having a housekeeper was great. I mean, we still [7] ______________ wash the dishes and keep things clean, but a housekeeper every week was good.

VOCABULARY

A Choose the best adjectives to complete the sentences.

1. Don't delay any more. Make your mind up. It's time to be ***decisive / aggressive***.
2. Stop yelling! You're being very ***effective / aggressive***.
3. He's very ***creative / competitive***. He hates losing.
4. eSports are already ***massive / expensive***. They'll definitely be in the Olympics soon.
5. You won 7–2? That's ***impressive / aggressive***!
6. Running with the ball is not very ***effective / competitive***. It's better to pass it quickly.

B Complete the text about sports with the missing words.

I loved my time as a soccer player. I only played for one club in the national [1]**l** e a g u e, but what a club! I had great [2]**c**_ _ _ _ _ _ who really improved my game, and our [3]**f**_ _ _ were amazing, always singing and cheering us on. It was a great feeling walking into the [4]**s**_ _ _ _ _ _, to hear that noise at the beginning of the game. And, of course, I played for the national team at three World Cup [5]**t**_ _ _ _ _ _ _ _ _ _, and the 2018 one was the highlight of my career. How can anything be better than winning the [6]**f**_ _ _ _ and lifting the [7]**t**_ _ _ _ _, knowing you are the [8]**c**_ _ _ _ _ _ _ _ _ of the world? I bet all the [9]**s**_ _ _ _ _ _ _ _ _ _ watching in the stadium and on TV were jealous! I think I can safely say I was a [10]**t**_ _ _ _ _ _ _ _ _. After all, I won the 'Player of the Year' award twice! I certainly miss those days. I don't get the same feeling from running a restaurant.

C Complete the radio vox-pop with the words in the box.

am	been	collect	get	joined	lost	took

Yes, I [1] ______________ stamps. I've [2] ______________ into stamp collecting for a long time. I [3] ______________ it up when I was just a kid. Some people think it is boring, but I have never [4] ______________ interest in it, and I'm 45 now. Of course, I [5] ______________ a member of my local stamp collecting society. I [6] ______________ that ten years ago. The weekly meetings [7] ______________ me out of the house.

FUNCTIONAL LANGUAGE

Complete the TV discussion with the correct phrases to express opinions.

Mario: Let's ask our panel of experts. You first, Tim, what do you think?

Tim: Well, in my [1] ______________, they should be banned.

Asif: If you [2] ______________ me, we shouldn't ban them.

Ana: As far as I'm [3] ______________, a ban is the answer.

Sue: I think we should do more research. Don't you [4] ______________?

Tim: To be [5] ______________, I disagree completely. We already know enough. To [6] ______________ you an example, there were five different stories about them in the newspapers last week.

7 FOOD

So long as you have food in your mouth, you have solved all questions for the time being.

Franz Kafka

Lunch in Marrakesh: Rainbow salad bowl, falafel and mint tea.

OBJECTIVES

- talk about eating out
- make speculations and deductions about food
- compare different types of food
- compare a range of solutions and choose the best one
- make suggestions
- write a reply in an online discussion forum

Work with a partner. Discuss the questions.

1 Look at the photo. How many types of food can you name?

2 Read the quote. What do you think it means?

3 Do you think it is important to eat with your family or friends? Why/Why not?

7.1 Eating out

- Talk about eating out
- Make speculations and deductions about food

P diphthongs; word stress with modals
G modals of speculation and deduction
V phrasal verbs; adjectives to describe food
S hidden contrasts

READING

A SPEAK Work in groups and discuss the questions.

1 Do you usually eat out in a restaurant? Why/Why not?

2 Do you usually leave a tip to thank the waiter for good service?

B READ FOR MAIN IDEA Read *Super supper clubs*. What are supper clubs? Why do many customers prefer supper clubs to traditional restaurants?

C Complete the notes on the differences between supper clubs and traditional restaurants. Use the strategies in the box to help you.

Paragraph	Supper clubs	Traditional restaurants
Choosing a dish (2)	*the chef chooses*	*you choose from a menu*
Where customers sit (2)		
Choosing when to go (2)		
What to cook (4)		
The food (4)		
The experience (5)		

Hidden contrasts

In articles about new or unusual things, writers frequently use words like *instead*, *just* and *even* to show contrasts with more normal things. These contrasts are usually hidden, so it's difficult to notice them. But they help you to understand the points that the writer wants to make.

SUPER SUPPER CLUBS

1 Anti-restaurants. Underground restaurants. Pop-up restaurants. Guestaurants. Whatever you call them, there's no doubt that supper clubs are one of the hottest trends in eating out today.

2 The idea is simple: instead of going to a traditional restaurant, you eat in the chef's home. Instead of choosing a dish from a menu, you eat what the chef gives you. And instead of sitting quietly at separate tables, all the customers eat together, talking and making friends. But if that sounds like your perfect evening, there's some bad news . You can't just show up when you're feeling hungry; you'll need to join a waiting list and then wait for an invitation from the chef.

3 The modern idea of supper clubs took off in Cuba in the 1990s. Cuba now has a huge amount of supper clubs, or *paladares*. Most of them started off as simply a room in the chef's home. They're popular with tourists, as well as people who want a simple home-cooked meal at a fair price. One of Cuba's best *paladares* is Castas y Tal, on the 11th floor of a large apartment building in central Havana. The main restaurant area has only eight seats, but there are wonderful views of the city below.

4 For chefs, supper clubs clearly seem like a great idea. They're fairly cheap and easy to set up because the chef can do everything at home. Instead of having to cook the same food again and again, supper clubs give chefs control over what to cook. Customers don't mind giving up some choice because they know they'll eat amazing food that they've never eaten before. They might not like it, but at least it won't be boring.

5 At the St. Jude Project in Mumbai, India, Chef Gresham Fernandes tries out ideas while he's cooking … and even while he's serving up the meal! He cooks in front of the guests, explaining what he's doing as he works.

6 So next time you're feeling adventurous, why not visit a supper club? It's sure to be an experience you won't forget!

PRONUNCIATION
Diphthongs

A Look at the underlined words in *Super supper clubs*. Match the words with their correct pronunciation (1–8). Then listen and check your answers.

7.1

1 weɪt ______
2 ju ______
3 dʒɔɪn ______
4 maɪt ______
5 hoʊm ______
6 daʊt ______
7 nuwz ______

B **WORK IT OUT** The words in Exercise A all contain diphthongs. Choose the best word or phrase to complete the rules.

Diphthongs

1 Diphthongs are long *vowel* / *consonant* sounds made from *two* / *three* short sounds.
2 We pronounce diphthongs by **moving quickly from one sound to the next / saying the two sounds separately**.
3 American English has *seven* / *ten* diphthongs: /eɪ/, /aɪ/, /oʊ/, /ɔɪ/, /aʊ/, /ju/, and /uw/.

C **SPEAK** Work in pairs. Make sentences using at least three of the words from Exercises A and B. Then practice saying your sentences.

VOCABULARY
Phrasal verbs

A Look at *Super supper clubs* again. Find sentences that have the same meaning as the ones below. Which words are used instead of the underlined words?

1 You can't just arrive without making a reservation when you're feeling hungry.
2 The modern idea of supper clubs really became popular in Cuba in the 1990s.
3 Most of them began their existence as simply a room in the chef's home.
4 They're fairly cheap and easy to get ready to start.
5 Customers don't mind losing some choice.
6 Chef Gresham Fernandes experiments with ideas while he's cooking … and even while he's putting the food on plates.

B **WORK IT OUT** Read the rules about phrasal verbs. Then complete the examples with phrasal verbs from Exercise A.

Phrasal verbs

1 Phrasal verbs are usually made of two parts: a verb (e.g. *work*, *try*) and a particle (e.g. *out*, *up*).
2 Sometimes it's possible to guess the meaning from the two words, but usually you just need to learn the meaning of the whole phrasal verb:
   - *You can't just* [a] ______ ______ *at their house! Always call first to check it's OK.*
3 Some phrasal verbs can have an object. When the object is short (e.g. a pronoun or one or two words), it usually comes in the middle:
   - *I have lots of ideas and I like to* [b] ______ *them* ______ *while I'm cooking.*

   But when the object is a longer phrase, it usually comes at the end:
   - *I like to* [c] ______ ______ *lots of new ideas while I'm cooking.*

C Go to the **Vocabulary Hub** on **page XVI**.

D **SPEAK** Complete the questions with the correct phrasal verbs. Then work in pairs and ask and answer the questions.

1 Do you think supper clubs will take ______ in your country?
2 Do you ever try ______ new meals while you're cooking or do you always plan carefully before you start?
3 Have your cooking skills ever let you ______? What went wrong?

SPEAKING

A Work in pairs. You are going to plan your own supper club. Write notes about:

- name
- location
- type of food
- cost
- number of guests
- what makes your supper club unique

B **PRESENT** Work in groups. Take turns presenting your supper club to the group.

C **REFLECT** Decide which supper club you would like to attend and why.

VOCABULARY

Adjectives to describe food

a

b

c

A Work in groups. Look at the pictures and discuss the questions.

1 Where do you think each dish is from?

2 What do you think it contains?

B Go to the **Vocabulary Hub** on **page XVII**.

C Many food adjectives end in *-y* (e.g. *spicy*). Complete the sentences with the missing adjectives. Use the words in bold to help you.

1 I didn't think this soup would **taste** very nice, but in fact it's really ___*tasty*___!

2 Honey is very ________. It **sticks** to the bread like glue!

3 I really love ________ pizza, so I always ask for extra **cheese** on the top.

4 This ________ sauce is too rich for me. How much **cream** did you put into it?

D SPEAK Work in pairs. Think of some types of food and drinks that these adjectives might describe. Use the glossary to help you.

buttery chocolatey fatty fruity oily meaty milky nutty peppery runny salty watery

E SPEAK Work in pairs. Use adjectives to describe:

1 your favorite soft drink.

2 your favorite flavor of ice cream.

3 your perfect breakfast.

4 your least favorite types of food.

LISTENING

A SPEAK Work in pairs. If you are invited to eat dinner at somebody's house, do you bring:

- flowers
- a gift
- something to drink
- dessert
- nothing

B Complete the description with the words in the box.

course dessert ~~dinner party~~ dishes host appetizer surprise

A [1] ___*dinner party*___ is an event where one person (the [2] ________) invites a group of friends to eat a meal at his or her house. At a traditional dinner party, the host cooks the food: an [3] ________ and a main [4] ________. But the guests usually bring something to drink, and perhaps also a [5] ________. In a pot luck dinner party, everybody (the host and guests) prepares one or two [6] ________. It's called pot luck because it's always a [7] ________: nobody knows what the others will bring.

7.2 **C** LISTEN FOR SPECIFIC INFORMATION Listen to a conversation at a pot luck dinner party. Match the people (1–5) with the dishes (a–e).

1	Vicky (the host)	a	cheesy chicken pasta surprise
2	Charlie	b	cream of chicken soup
3	Tina	c	spicy buffalo wings
4	Felipe	d	cheese and chilli salad
5	Markus	e	chicken curry in a creamy sauce

Glossary

allergic (adj) affected by an allergy (a medical condition in which you become sick or your skin becomes covered with red marks as a reaction to something you eat, breathe or touch)

buffalo (n) a large African animal similar to a cow, with curved horns

dairy products (n) foods that are made from milk (e.g. cheese, butter, ice cream)

spicy (adj) food that has a strong hot flavor

7.2 **D** Listen again. Check (✓) the correct name(s).

	Vicky	Charlie	Felipe	Tina	Markus
1 Who arrived late?					
2 Whose dish needs to be heated up?					
3 Who is allergic to dairy products?					
4 Who doesn't like spicy food?					
5 Who doesn't like chicken?					

E SPEAK Work in groups and discuss the questions.

1 What went wrong with the pot luck dinner party?
2 Does it matter if some things go wrong at a party like this?

GRAMMAR
Modals of speculation and deduction

A WORK IT OUT Choose the correct meaning for the sentences from the conversation at the pot luck dinner party.

1 They **can't be** buffalo wings. Buffaloes don't have wings!
  a Maybe they aren't buffalo wings.
  b I'm sure they aren't buffalo wings.
2 They **could be** chicken or something like that.
  a It's possible that they're chicken.
  b It was possible that they were chicken.
3 You **must think** I'm so disorganized!
  a I'm sure you think this.
  b It's necessary for you to think this.
4 Well, they **might not be** chilies.
  a It isn't possible that they're chilies.
  b Maybe they aren't chilies.
5 Uh … you **may have** a problem there.
  a Maybe you have a problem.
  b I'm sure you have a problem.

B Look again at the sentences in Exercise A. Complete the rules (1–4) with the words in the box.

Modals of speculation and deduction

can't could may may not might might not must

1 We use ______________ when we are sure something is true.
2 We use ______________, ______________ or ______________ when we think something is possibly true, but we are not sure.
3 We use ______________ or ______________ when we think something possibly isn't true, but we are not sure.
4 We use ______________ when we are sure something is not true.

C Go to the **Grammar Hub** on **page VIII**.

PRONUNCIATION
Word stress with modals

7.3 **A** Listen to the sentences (1–4) from the conversation at the pot luck dinner party. Then match the sentences with the rules (a–d).

1 Oh, that must be Felipe, right?
2 Hang on … that can't be right.
3 The name must come from the city, not the animal.
4 They might not be chilies.

a We usually place extra stress on the word *not* or a negative modal verb. ___, ___
b Modal verb + *be*: We usually stress the modal verb, not *be*. ___, ___
c Modal verb + main verb: We usually stress both verbs about the same. ___
d When we're speaking quickly, we usually don't pronounce the *t* in *must*. ___, ___

7.4 **B** Look at the highlighted words in the sentences below and underline the stressed words. Then listen and check your answers.

1 You're such a great host. You must have a lot of dinner parties!
2 'What's wrong with the oven?' 'I don't know. It might not be turned on.'
3 I made a lot of soup because some people may want two or three bowls.
4 Oh, no! Felipe can't be here already! The party doesn't start for another 20 minutes!

7.4 **C** Listen again and repeat the sentences. Then work in pairs and practice saying the sentences. Listen and check your partner's pronunciation.

D SPEAK Work in pairs. Make deductions and speculations about the people at the dinner party. Think about these questions.

1 How do they know each other?
2 What is the surprise in Tina's cheesy chicken pasta surprise?

SPEAKING HUB

A You have been invited to a pot luck dinner party. Write a short description of the dish you would like to bring.

B SPEAK Work in groups. Choose one person to be the host and give him/her your description. In your groups, decide:

- who brought which dish.
- which dishes you want to try.

C REFLECT Tell the class about your pot luck dinner party. Which dishes were the most popular?

- Talk about eating out
- Make speculations and deductions about food

7.2 Food fads

- Compare different types of food
- Compare a range of solutions and choose the best one

G comparatives and superlatives; *the …, the …* **P** vowel + *w* **V** waste **S** identifying people's opinions

READING

A SPEAK Read the definition of *fad*. Then work in pairs and discuss the questions.

> **fad** – definition and synonyms
> NOUN Pronunciation /fæd/
> 1 something that is popular or fashionable for only a short time

1 Can you think of any current food fads? Which foods are fashionable now?
2 Are there any food fads connected with different ways of cooking? Or different ways of eating?
3 Which older food fads have gone out of fashion?

B READ FOR GIST Read *Food fads* quickly. What is the writer's opinion about superfoods?

a They're just a fad – they aren't really very good for you.
b Expensive superfoods are much healthier than cheaper food.
c You don't need to spend a lot of money to buy some superfoods.
d Most superfoods are actually bad for your health.

FOOD FADS

Hi again! This week, I've decided to look at one of the biggest food fads of the 21st century: superfoods. Let's try to sort the facts from the fiction!

Quinoa has a long history as a superfood: it was known to the ancient Incas as 'the mother of all grains' because it was so healthy. Even today it's recommended by NASA as the perfect food for long space flights. Like all whole grains, it can help your body fight a variety of diseases, and it contains lots of vitamins, minerals and fiber. It's also one of the best sources of protein, so it's perfect for vegetarians and vegans, too. Amazing!

Goji berries are another great source of plant-based protein. These sweet berries have been used in China for centuries as a way to protect against illness. They contain less sugar than other fruits, so they're one of the healthiest snacks around. Unfortunately, they can be dangerous for some people, so always check with your doctor before eating them.

Açaí berries are perhaps the most successful superfoods of all: not long ago, they were unknown outside of Brazil. Now, açaí products are big business. Why are they so popular? Well, some people believe these berries will help them to grow old more slowly … or even to live longer. Like goji berries, they're full of chemicals which seem to protect our hearts and our brains. Sounds good, right?

Chia seeds are known as the healthiest food on the planet. The name 'chia' comes from the ancient Mayan word for 'strength'. Out of all the foods in the world, chia seeds contain some of the most nutrients for the fewest calories. They're also one of the best sources of fiber, which is great for your digestive system. Even better, they make you feel full … so you'll eat fewer snacks!

C READ FOR SPECIFIC INFORMATION Read again. Write *A* (açaí berries), *B* (broccoli), *C* (chia seeds), *G* (goji berries) or *Q* (quinoa).

According to the blog post, which superfood ...

1 isn't only eaten on our planet? ___
2 is much cheaper than other superfoods? ___
3 might help you stay younger for longer? ___
4 can help you digest your food more effectively? ___
5 might not be safe for everybody? ___
6 has become popular very quickly? ___
7 helps you to eat less food between meals? ___

D SPEAK Work in groups and discuss the questions.

1 Do you think it's worth paying more money for superfoods? Why/Why not?
2 Do you think it is more important for you to eat healthy food or tasty food? Why?
3 What are some simple ways that we can eat more healthily?

But before you all rush out to buy superfoods from your local health food store, remember that superfoods are usually super expensive, too! And do you know what? Strawberries are probably just as good for you as goji berries and açaí berries. Similarly, quinoa and chia seeds are great because they're whole grains. But you can get all that fiber far more cheaply by eating plenty of brown bread, brown rice and whole grain pasta. And what's the best superfood of all? Broccoli! It's cheap, tasty and incredibly good for you. It isn't as exciting as quinoa, but it's a lot less expensive!

Glossary

fiber (n) the parts of fruit, vegetables and grains that your body cannot digest (= turn into substances it can use); it helps food to pass through your body

nutrient (n) a substance in food that plants, animals and people need to live and grow

protein (n) a substance in food, such as meat, eggs and milk, that people need in order to grow and be healthy

GRAMMAR

Comparatives and superlatives

A Cover the *Food fads* article. Complete the sentences with one word in each space. Then check your answers in the blog post.

1 This week, I've decided to look at one of ___*the*___ biggest food fads of the 21st century: superfoods.
2 They contain ________ sugar ________ other fruits, so they're one of ________ healthiest snacks around.
3 Chia seeds contain some of the ________ nutrients for the ________ calories.
4 Even better, they make you feel full ... so you'll eat ________ snacks!
5 Some people believe these berries will help them to grow old ________ slowly ... or even to live ________.
6 It isn't ________ exciting ________ quinoa, but it's a lot ________ expensive!

B Go to the Grammar Hub on page VIII.

C SPEAK Work in pairs. Compare each set of ideas.

1 quinoa vs white rice
2 broccoli vs ice cream
3 grocery stores vs health food stores
4 fast food vs superfoods
5 cooking vs eating out
6 eating alone vs eating in a large group

A: Quinoa is much tastier than white rice.
B: Yes, but it's a lot more expensive.

SPEAKING

Work in pairs. Use the superlative form of the words and phrases in the box to ask and answer questions.

bad expensive far (to travel for a meal) few ingredients little money (to spend on food) much time (to spend preparing a meal) spicy

A: What's the farthest you've ever traveled for a meal?
B: Not very far. I usually buy all my food in the local store. But once I spent an hour bike riding to the 'best ice cream store in town'. But it wasn't as good as I expected.

LISTENING

A Work in pairs. Take the **Reduce Your Waste** quiz. Then go to the **Communication Hub** on **page XX** to check your answers.

7.5 **B** You are going to listen to part of a radio show about a family who is trying to waste less food. Look at the pictures (1–6) and guess the answers to the questions. Then listen and check your answers.

REDUCE YOUR WASTE

1 How long can you store these things before they go bad?

a fresh milk in a fridge
b frozen vegetables in a freezer
c fresh bananas
d dry food (e.g. pasta)
e an opened bottle of apple juice in a fridge
f a plate of leftovers in a fridge

2 True or false?

a You can safely reheat food as many times as you like.
b Most food is still safe to eat after it has passed its best if used by date.
c You must eat rice within 24 hours of cooking it.

1 How much money does the average person lose from food waste every year?

2 Do ugly carrots taste as good as beautiful carrots?

3 What's the problem with growing lettuce in a greenhouse?

4 How many buckets of water does it take to make a loaf of bread?

5 What can you do with your leftovers if you don't want to waste them?

6 How can a cell phone app help us waste less food?

C Who expressed each of these opinions: *Mrs. Taylor*, *Mr. Taylor*, *Alison* or *Philip*? Use the strategies in the box to help you.

Identifying people's opinions

When you're listening, pay attention to whether people are just describing a situation or expressing an opinion about it. Adjectives like *great* and *awful* usually show that the person is expressing an opinion.

1 Food doesn't need to be beautiful. Mrs. Taylor
2 I like collecting and studying detailed information about our experiment. ________
3 Food waste is bad for our planet. ________
4 I didn't like eating the same food the next day. ________
5 I enjoy cooking meals to use up the food in the fridge. ________
6 Money isn't the most important reason for reducing waste. ________

D **SPEAK** Work in pairs. How much food do you think you waste in your family?

GRAMMAR

the …, the …

A **WORK IT OUT** Look at the sentences from the radio show. Match the beginnings of the sentences (1–5) with the endings (a–e).

1 The more I researched the topic,
2 The less food we throw away,
3 The less we cook,
4 The longer we do it,
5 The more carefully you count things,

a the more normal it feels.
b the better.
c the more I realized that we aren't just throwing away food.
d the more accurate your results will be.
e the less we waste.

B Read the rule and complete the example. Use the words in parentheses to help you.

the …, the …

To show that two changes are closely connected, we use ***the*** + comparative, ***the*** + comparative. As one thing changes, it makes the other thing change.

As far as I'm concerned, the ________ (ugly), the ________ (good)!

C Go to the **Grammar Hub** on **page VIII**.

PRONUNCIATION

Vowel + *w*

7.6 **A** How do you pronounce these words? Use the strategies in the box to help you. Then listen and repeat the words.

chew cow own raw stew

Vowel + *w*

Three vowels, ***a***, ***e*** and ***o***, when combined with ***w***, make a new sound. There are two possible sounds for ***e*** + ***w*** and ***o*** + ***w***.

a + *w* **/ɔː/** for, draw, awful, ______________, ______________

e + *w* **/juː/** you, few, view, ______________

e + *w* **/uː/** too, jewelry, threw, ______________, ______________

o + *w* **/oʊ/** go, low, owe, ______________, ______________, ______________, ______________, ______________

o + *w* **/aʊ/** out, how, wow, ______________, ______________, ______________

7.7 **B** Look at the bold words in these sentences. Write them in the correct place in the box in Exercise A. Then listen and check your answers.

1 'Have you ever **flown** in a helicopter?' 'Yes, I **flew** in one a **few** weeks ago. It was **awesome**.'

2 You aren't **allowed** to **throw** away your trash here! Don't you **know** it's against the **law**!

3 The **flowers grew** fairly **slowly** at first, but **now** they're fully **grown**.

C SPEAK Work in pairs. Practice saying the sentences in Exercise B. Listen and check your partner's pronunciation.

VOCABULARY

Waste

A Match the definitions (1–8) with the words and phrases in the box.

garbage can cut down get rid of recycle reduce reuse garbage throw away use up ~~waste~~

1 to not use something that you could use ______ *waste*

2 a container for putting garbage in ______________

3 things that you throw away because they are no longer useful ______________

4 to use all of something, so there's no waste ______________

5 to change waste materials such as newspapers and bottles so that they can be used again ______________

6 to use something again ______________

7 to use less of something ______________, ______________

8 to get rid of something that you no longer want ______________, ______________

B SPEAK Complete the questions with one word in each space. Then work in pairs and discuss the questions.

1 Do you ______________ plastic and glass containers so they can be turned into new products, or do you just get ______________ of them?

2 Do you ______________ plastic bags again and again, or throw them in the ______________?

3 How could restaurants cut ______________ the amount of ______________ they throw ______________ each week?

SPEAKING HUB

A Work in pairs. How could you reduce food waste in your home by fifty percent? Write notes about:

- shopping habits (how often? how much?)
- meal planning (weekly menus)
- leftovers
- food storage (fridge? cupboard? special containers?)
- apps and gadgets

B PRESENT Use your notes to prepare a short presentation on how you can help people reduce their food waste. Present your ideas to the class.

C DISCUSS Work in groups. Use these questions to compare your ideas from Exercise B. Then choose the best two or three ideas.

- Which ideas will be easiest for people to understand and follow?
- Which ideas will make the biggest difference?
- Which ideas might cost people more money? Which ideas might save them money?

D REFLECT Work in groups and discuss the questions.

1 Are you going to try to reduce your own food waste? How?

2 Will you try to persuade others to cut their food waste? How?

- Compare different types of food
- Compare a range of solutions and choose the best one

Café Hub

7.3 Comfort eating

F – make suggestions   P – suggestions

COMPREHENSION

A Work in pairs and discuss the questions.

What do you do when you're feeling upset or worried?

Do you cook, go for a run, call a friend, watch a good movie or something else?

B ▶ 00:00–01:30 Watch the first part of the video and answer the questions.

1 What is Gaby's big news?
2 What does Milly think about her news?
3 What is Gaby upset about?

C ▶ 00:56–01:21 Find and correct five mistakes in the story that Gaby told Milly. What advice do you think Milly will give? Watch to check your answers.

It was about a week ago. Last Wednesday, Sam had to leave work early and so he asked me to look after the café. I had decided to tell him how I felt, and so before I locked up, I wrote a poem expressing my true feelings for him. ... And I left it on the doormat for him to find. He can't have seen it.

FUNCTIONAL LANGUAGE

Making suggestions

A Match the two halves of the extracts from the video.

Making a suggestion

1 Have you tried
2 What about
3 The best thing might be
4 If I were you, I'd
5 Why don't we
6 We could

a cook something delicious.
b take some time to think about it.
c talking to him about it?
d put on some whipped cream and sprinkles?
e sending a text or an email or something?
f to just ask him if he got the letter.

B Complete the phrases in the table.

Saying no to a suggestion	Saying yes to a suggestion
No, I ________. I don't know what to say.	That's a good ________.
No, that wouldn't ________. To say what?	It's worth a ________.
That's a ________ idea. I'm already really embarrassed.	Good ________.

C ▶ 01:21–04:13 Watch the second part of the video and check your answers to Exercises A and B.

MILLY

SAM

NEENA

ZAC

GABY

USEFUL PHRASES

A Match the useful phrases (1–4) with the screenshots (a–d).

1 What's up? ___
2 Great timing! ___
3 It'll help take your mind off Sam. ___
4 He's been acting like nothing happened! ___

a

b

c

d

B How do you say these useful phrases in your language?

PRONUNCIATION

Suggestions

7.8 **A** Listen to the extracts from the video and underline the stressed/key words. Does the intonation rise or fall at the end of each phrase?

Milly: Have you tried talking to him about it?
Gaby: No, I can't. I don't know what to say.
Milly: Or, what about sending him a text or an email or something?
Gaby: No, that wouldn't work. To say what?
Milly: I don't know exactly. The best thing might be to just ask him if he got the letter?
Gaby: No, no, no, no, no, no, no, no! That's a terrible idea. I'm already really embarrassed.
Milly: If I were you, I'd take some time to think about it.

B In pairs, practice the conversation. Copy the stress and intonation.

SPEAKING

A Work in pairs. Think about possible solutions to the problems below.

1 I'm having a dinner party, but I hate cooking.
2 I want to eat more healthily, but superfoods are too expensive.
3 I want to save some money, but I love going out to restaurants!
4 I frequently have leftover food, but I don't want to waste it.
5 I want to grow vegetables, but I live in an apartment.

B DISCUSS Take turns reading out a problem and make suggestions using the phrases in Functional Language Exercise A.

A: I'm having a dinner party, but I hate cooking.
B: What about getting takeout?

Make suggestions

➤ Turn to page XXV to learn how to write a reply in an online discussion forum.

Unit 7 Review

GRAMMAR

A Choose the best words to complete the conversation.

A: Do you want some of this pot luck stew? I made it from all of last week's leftovers: fish curry, cheesy chicken pasta, spicy vegetables ...

B: Yuck! That [1]***can't / might not / must*** taste disgusting!

A: Well, no, it actually tastes very good. Try it – you [2]***can / might / must*** like it.

B: Really? OK. I guess it [3]***couldn't / might not / must not*** be so bad. But don't forget I'm allergic to peanuts.

A: Don't worry, it [4]***can't / may not / might*** contain any peanuts. I never cook with them. But it [5] ***couldn't / may / must*** contain some other types of nuts – I'm not sure. Is that OK?

B: Yes, that's fine. Hmm ... this [6]***can't / could / must*** be a big mistake, but ... OK, I'll try it.

B Complete the sentences with the correct form of the words in parentheses.

1 I want to cook the most food for the ______________________ (*little*) money. Any ideas?

2 Açaí berries are really good for you – they're much ______________________ (*healthy*) than I thought.

3 If you want to lose weight, you need to eat ______________________ (*few*) candy.

4 You should come to the restaurant on a Tuesday at lunchtime – that's the ______________________ (*crowded*) time.

5 You baked this cake too quickly! Next time, try baking it ______________________ (*slowly*).

6 Cooking for ten people is far ______________________ (*stressful*) than cooking for one!

7 There's too much cream in this sauce. Can you make it a little ______________________ (*creamy*) next time?

C Match the beginnings of the sentences (1–6) with the endings (a–f).

1 Bring all your friends to our dinner party – the more people who come,

2 The earlier you arrive at the restaurant,

3 The older I get,

4 The more sugar you add,

5 Natural food is much better for you; the fewer chemicals it contains,

6 Don't boil vegetables for too long; the longer you cook them,

a the more I prefer to stay in and cook at home.

b the less flavor they'll have.

c the more fun we'll have.

d the more likely you are to get a table.

e the sweeter it will be.

f the healthier it is.

VOCABULARY

A Complete the sentences with the correct form of the phrasal verbs in the box.

keep on clean up end up put off figure out

1 I can't ______________ how to turn on the microwave. Can you help me?

2 Sorry to interrupt your meal, but I need to go out for a minute. Please ______________ eating while I'm away.

3 I'm happy to cook dinner, but could you ______________ the dirty plates afterward?

4 If you want to learn to cook, don't ______________ it ______________! Join our cooking classes today!

5 I was planning to cook a big meal, but then the oven broke so I ______________ buying takeout pizzas for everybody.

B Choose the best adjectives to complete the sentences.

1 I think we need to cook this meat a little longer – it's still ***delicious / mild / raw*** in the middle.

2 I don't really like sweet snacks. Do you have anything ***bitter / rich / savory***, like a sandwich?

3 Don't worry. This soup is very ***buttery / mild / spicy*** – there are no chilies or strong flavors in it.

4 The food was great, but it wasn't very ***chewy / filling / spicy***. We were still hungry at the end of the meal!

5 I don't like dark chocolate – it's too ***fatty / bitter / creamy*** for me. I prefer something sweeter.

6 If you want a cheap and ***disgusting / sour / tasty*** lunch, Kate's café is the best place to go.

C Complete the advice about food waste with words in the box. There is one extra word.

garbage cans get recycle reduce reuse throw use

Try these tips:

- Don't [1]____________ rid of yesterday's bread just because it isn't fresh. Make toast to [2]____________ up the last few pieces.
- Don't [3]____________ old plastic away. You can [4]____________ the same shopping bags again and again.
- Use two (or more) [5]____________: one for food waste and one for containers that you can [6]____________.

FUNCTIONAL LANGUAGE

Find and correct the mistakes in the sentences.

1 I don't feel like cooking tonight. Why ~~we~~ don't ^we eat out tonight?

2 Yes, why not? What about go to The Food Zone?

____

3 Again? We went there last week. Could we going to that new supper club, The Spicy Kitchen, instead?

____

4 Good idea! The best thing might be call them. They might have a free table tonight.

____

5 Yes, that's worth to try. Can you call them and ask?

____

8 INNOVATION

To invent, you need a good imagination and a pile of junk.

Thomas Edison

A helicopter mechanic double checks some wiring, Germany.

OBJECTIVES

- explain how an invention works
- suggest and evaluate creative ideas
- use positive language to promote a new product
- give a friend advice about choosing a gadget
- give and follow instructions
- write a biography

Work with a partner. Discuss the questions.

1 Look at the picture. What characteristics would be helpful to have as a mechanic?

2 Look at the quote. Do you think you have to be imaginative to be an inventor?

3 Talk about a situation where you have been imaginative or innovative in your life.

8.1 Making a difference

- Explain how an invention works
- Suggest and evaluate creative ideas

V – word families; creative thinking G – adjective clauses P – adjective clauses
S – listening for problems and solutions

Eden Full Goh:

the inventor who is making a big difference

Eden Full Goh is perhaps not a name that you immediately recognize, but she is one of the most exciting and creative inventors of the 21st century.

Eden, who was born in Calgary, Canada, started to show talent at the age of nine, when she built a solar-powered toy car. That is where her interest in solar power began but certainly not where it stopped. She had not yet graduated from college when she came up with a very simple, but highly efficient, solar panel system that produces energy at low cost.

Eden's invention, which has won many prizes, is now used in 19 countries, where it makes a real difference to thousands of people's lives. Here is how to use it.

1. The SunSaluter is like a table. The top of the table is a solar panel, which can face in different directions.
2. Get up early in the morning when it's still dark. Fill one plastic bottle with sand and two more bottles with dirty water.
3. Attach the water bottles to the filter. At the bottom of the filter is a tube that takes clean water to a large container. At the top there's a hook that attaches the filter to the SunSaluter.
4. Hang the filter on one end of the SunSaluter, which will then go down. Hang the bottle that you filled with sand on the other end of the solar panel. Make sure the solar panel is facing the east, where the sun will rise.
5. At sunrise, when the sun comes up, the solar panel will start catching sunlight from the east.
6. During the day, the water will flow very slowly through the filter to the container, where it is stored. As the water bottles become lighter, the heavy sand bottle slowly pulls the other end of the SunSaluter down. At noon, when the sun is high in the sky, the solar panel will face upwards.
7. In the evening, when the water bottles are empty, the solar panel will face west. You can now drink the clean water that you collected during the day.

Glossary

solar panel (n) a piece of equipment that uses energy from the sun to create power

READING

A SPEAK Work in pairs and discuss the questions.

1. What famous inventors do you know? What did they invent?
2. What skills do inventors need?

B READ FOR GIST Read *Eden Full Goh: the inventor who is making a big difference*. What is special about Eden and her invention?

C READ FOR DETAIL Read again. Match the explanations (1–7) in the text with the pictures (a–g).

D SPEAK Make a list of your own life goals. Use the ideas in the box to help you. Then work in pairs and compare your lists.

awards and prizes career experiences family helping other people certifications

VOCABULARY

Word families

A Read the box. Then complete the word families. Use *Eden Full Goh: the inventor who is making a big difference* to help you.

Word families

Word families can help you learn many words together, not just one at a time. Here's an example:

innovation (n) = a new idea or product

innovator (n) = someone who thinks of new ideas or products

innovate (v) = to invent or begin using new ideas or products

innovative (adj) = an adjective to describe an innovator or an innovation

Noun (thing/idea)	Noun (person)	Verb	Adjective
a success	a success	to succeed (in something)	1 successful
an 2 ______	an 3 ______	to invent something	inventive
a design	a designer	to 4 ______ something	–
a product	a producer	to 5 ______ something	productive
6 ______	a scientist	–	scientific
engineering	an 7 ______	to engineer something	–

B Complete the sentences with words from the same family as the words in bold.

1 You don't need to be **successful** every time. You just need to *succeed* in the most important things.

2 I could never **invent** something – I'm not a very ________ person.

3 You can only call yourself an ________ after studying **engineering** in college.

4 A ________ should concentrate on **designing** things that work well. That's more important than making them look beautiful.

5 I always think like a **scientist**. Being ________ means checking the facts before making a decision, and not focusing on opinions and feelings.

C SPEAK Work in pairs. Which sentences in Exercise B do you agree or disagree with? Tell your partner. Then make the sentences true for you.

GRAMMAR
Adjective clauses

A WORK IT OUT Look at *Eden Full Goh: the inventor who is making a big difference.* What do the highlighted words in the article refer to?

1 who	= *Eden*	4 which	= ________
2 when	= ________	5 that	= ________
3 where	= ________		

B Read the rules and complete the examples with adjective clauses from the article.

Adjective clauses

Essential adjective clauses tell us which person, thing, place or time we are talking about. Without the adjective clause, the sentence isn't complete.

Eden Full Goh: the inventor [1] ________.

Non-essential adjective clauses give extra information about a person, thing, place or time. We can cut the adjective clause and the sentence is still complete. We use commas to separate the adjective clause from the rest of the sentence.

Eden's invention, [2] ________, is now used in 19 countries.

C Go to the Grammar Hub on page X.

PRONUNCIATION
Adjective clauses

A 8.1 Listen to the two sentences. What do you notice about the pronunciation of essential adjective clauses and non-essential adjective clauses?

1 The person who invented the SunSaluter has made a big difference to people's lives.

2 Eden Full Goh, who invented the SunSaluter, has made a big difference to people's lives.

B 8.2 Listen and repeat the sentences.

1 Solar panels, which turn sunlight into electricity, are becoming cheaper all the time.

2 I've hidden my plans in a place where they'll be safe.

3 My favorite inventor is Mária Telkes, who created the first 100 percent solar-powered house in 1947.

C SPEAK Work in pairs. Practice saying the sentences in Exercise B. Listen and check your partner's pronunciation.

SPEAKING

A Work in pairs. Write down three sentences using adjective clauses. They should describe:

- a famous person
- a place
- an object

B Join another pair and take turns reading out your sentences, saying 'Beep' in place of the subject. The other pair must guess who, where or what you are talking about.

A: Beep, who is American, invented the light bulb.
B: Is it Thomas Edison?

Thinking outside THE BOX

Thinking outside the box means looking at a problem in a new way. It means forgetting about 'the way we normally do things', taking away unimportant rules and experimenting with new ideas. So for example, in the 'nine dots' problem, we see 'rules' that don't actually exist. Who said your lines have to stay inside the red box? In fact, do the lines even need to go through the middle of each dot?

It's the same with the light bulb problem. We can't stop ourselves from thinking of a light bulb as something that we see with our eyes, as something that can only be in two states, off or on. But what if we think of it as something we can touch with our hands? Are there still only two states?

Thinking outside the box also helps with brainstorming tasks, like the 'uses for old tickets' exercise. The key to successful brainstorming is to break it into two stages: generating ideas in the first place, and then evaluating those ideas to see if they're useful or not. We need to keep those stages separate; if we try to do both at the same time, we only generate boring, sensible ideas. But sometimes it's the silly ideas that help us to find excellent ideas. For example, a single bus ticket wouldn't make a great poster for your wall, but what about a poster made from 100 bus tickets from around the world?

READING

A SPEAK Work in pairs. How creative are you? Follow the instructions to find out.

1. Take an object from your pocket/bag (e.g. a used bus ticket). Try to think of as many different uses as possible for this object. Your ideas can be sensible or silly. What's your best idea?
   A: We could cut it up to make a tiny jigsaw puzzle.
   B: Why don't we write a short shopping list on the back?
2. Draw four straight lines to connect all the dots without taking your pen off the page. Now try again with only three straight lines.

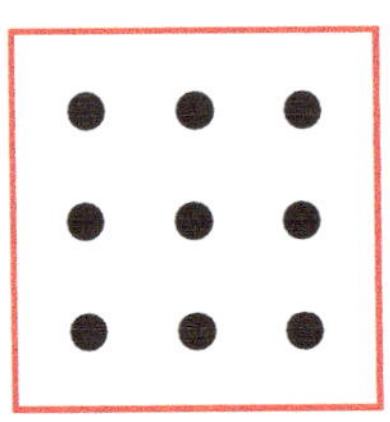

3. You're inside a room with three light switches on the wall. One of these switches turns on a light in a room on the other side of the house, but you don't know which switch. How can you find out? You can go to the other room to check only once.

B READ FOR GIST Read *Thinking outside the box.* How does it help with the questions in Exercise A?

C READ FOR DETAIL Choose *Do* or *Don't* for each piece of advice.

1. *Do / Don't* look at a problem in a new way.
2. *Do / Don't* do things the way you normally do them.
3. *Do / Don't* experiment with new ideas.
4. *Do / Don't* guess the rules and follow those rules.
5. *Do / Don't* evaluate ideas while you're generating them.

D SPEAK Work in groups. When do you need to brainstorm ideas? How could brainstorming silly ideas help you to think of useful ideas?

LISTENING

A SPEAK Work in pairs. The pictures show some techniques for becoming more creative. What do you think the techniques are?

8.3 **B LISTEN FOR GIST** Listen to a conversation between two friends, Caroline and Toby, to check your answers to Exercise A. Number the pictures in the order they are mentioned.

Glossary

wander (v) if your mind or thoughts wander, you stop concentrating and start thinking about other things

8.3 **C Listen again. What was the solution to each problem? Use the strategies in the box to help you.**

> **Listening for problems and solutions**
>
> When you're listening, it's useful to organize information into a set of problems and solutions. This usually makes it easier to understand a lot of information and to remember it better later.
>
> Listen carefully when you hear people talking about problems because they'll probably present a solution next.

1 You don't learn how to be creative at school.
  - a Write stories and design clothes.
  - b Go to creativity classes.
  - c Read books about creativity.

2 You're too busy to stop working.
  - a Take a break to make yourself more productive.
  - b Work in the evenings so you can have a break during the day.
  - c Relax – your work isn't as important as you think.

3 Your brain is filled with too much information.
  - a Get some physical exercise.
  - b Watch TV and play games on your phone.
  - c Turn off your computer.

4 You need to think outside the box.
  - a Go to the library to get some ideas.
  - b Look at blue things.
  - c Listen to some music.

5 You have no ideas at all.
  - a Discuss your ideas with a group of friends.
  - b Close your eyes for a few minutes.
  - c Use letters of the alphabet to generate ideas.

D SPEAK Work in pairs. Which of Caroline's techniques have you used? Which might you use in the future? Tell your partner.

VOCABULARY
Creative thinking

A Match the beginnings of the sentences (1–10) with the endings (a–j).

1 I'm terrible at **coming up**
2 You can actually learn to **use your**
3 A break actually **boosted my**
4 You need to **unplug**
5 You need to **let your mind**
6 They're all good for **generating**
7 Whenever I need to **think outside**
8 You're letting your emotions **block**
9 You should **look at a problem**
10 My mind's

a **the box**, I go to the beach.
b **wander freely**.
c **imagination** better.
d **your creativity**.
e **gone blank**.
f **creativity**.
g **with new ideas**.
h **from the outside**.
i **completely**.
j **new ideas**.

B Look at the sentences in Exercise A. What do the phrases in bold mean?

C SPEAK Choose the best words to complete the questions. Then work in groups and ask and answer the questions.

1 Does your mind ever *boost* / *generate* / *wander* during boring activities? Think of some examples.
2 Is it possible to *come up* / *unplug* / *block* completely from the things that make you stressed? How can you do it?
3 What can you do when your *mind* / *creativity* / *imagination* goes blank in a stressful situation (e.g. when you're in an exam, giving a presentation or speaking English)?

SPEAKING HUB

A Work in groups. You have decided to create a website that will make a big difference to people's lives. Use the alphabet technique to generate some ideas – silly or serious!

Write down three letters of the alphabet.
- 1st letter: Who is your website for?
- 2nd letter: What problem do those people have?
- 3rd letter: How will you solve that problem?

B PLAN Think of five ideas for each of the questions below. Remember to think outside the box!

1 What will you call your website?
2 How can you make money from your website?
3 How will you tell the world about your website?

C ORGANIZE Look at your ideas from Exercise B. Turn your silly ideas into excellent ideas. Choose your best idea.

D PRESENT Present your idea to the class. Which teams' websites would you visit?

- Explain how an invention works
- Suggest and evaluate creative ideas

8.2 Must-have gadgets

- Use positive language to promote a new product
- Give a friend advice about choosing a gadget

V positive adjectives
P *'ll* and *won't*
G zero and first conditionals; conditionals with modals and imperatives
S topic sentences

LISTENING

A SPEAK Work in pairs. Look at the pictures of inventions (a–d) and discuss the questions.

1 What do you think the gadgets in the pictures do?
2 How useful are they?
3 Do you like gadgets? What gadgets do you own?

8.4 **B LISTEN FOR MAIN IDEA** Listen to a podcast about new gadgets and answer the questions.

1 Which gadgets from the pictures do the people discuss?
2 What is special about them?

8.4 **C** Listen again. Which gadgets do these sentences describe? Write *O* (Oombrella), *C* (CleverPet) or *B* (both).

1 It looks beautiful. ___
2 It's connected to the internet. ___
3 It sends messages to your phone. ___
4 It's useful for many years. ___
5 It gets more difficult to use over time. ___
6 It can lead to a longer life. ___

D SPEAK Work in groups and discuss the questions.

1 What is good about the two gadgets? Which one is more useful?
2 Who do you think will buy the gadgets? Why?

VOCABULARY

Positive adjectives

Using positive adjectives

As your English improves, try to avoid using words like *good* or *nice* too frequently. There are many other positive words that you can use like *amazing*, *excellent* and *wonderful*.

A Match the positive adjectives (1–10) with the meanings (a–j).

1 gorgeous
2 sensible
3 practical
4 unforgettable
5 impressive
6 unique
7 sophisticated
8 incredible
9 suitable
10 fascinating

a you admire it because it is very good, large or shows great skill
b making you very interested or attracted
c right for a particular purpose, person or situation
d not the same as anything or anyone else
e reasonable and practical
f will be remembered for a very long time
g surprising, or difficult to believe
h very beautiful
i complicated and advanced in design
j intended to be useful

B Go to the **Vocabulary Hub** on **page XVII**.

C SPEAK Work in pairs. Write down the names of your favorite three possessions. Use positive adjectives to tell your partner why you like each one. Ask questions about your partner's possessions.

a

b

GRAMMAR

Zero and first conditionals

8.5 **A** **Look at the extracts from the podcast about new gadgets. Match the beginnings of the sentences (1–4) with the endings (a–d). Then listen and check your answers.**

1 I never go for a walk
2 Will it keep me dry
3 If this Oombrella lasts for years,
4 Pets stay healthier and they live longer

a if there's a storm tomorrow morning?
b if they keep busy.
c I'll be very happy.
d unless the sun's shining.

B WORK IT OUT **Choose the correct words to complete the rules.**

Zero and first conditional

1 Conditional sentences usually have ***two / four*** clauses: the *if*-clause and the result clause.
2 When the *if*-clause comes first, we ***always / never*** need a comma between the clauses.
3 We can use ***unless*** instead of ***if***. It means ***if not / because***.
4 We use the zero conditional to talk about things that are always true. We use ***past / present*** tenses in both clauses.
5 We use the first conditional to talk about possible situations in the ***future / past***. We usually use ***will*** in the result clause.

C Go to the Grammar Hub on page X.

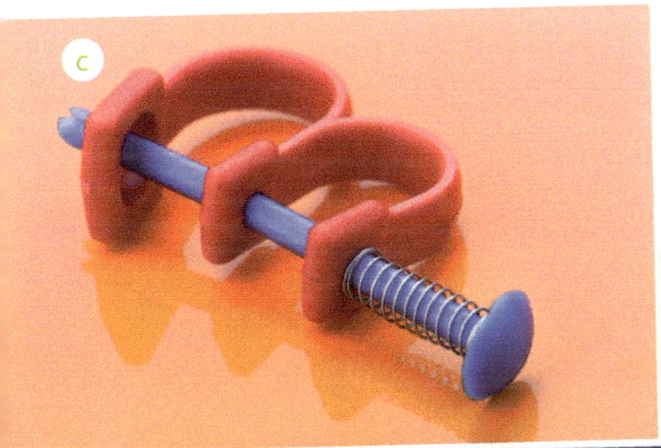

PRONUNCIATION

'll and *won't*

'll* and *won't

It's sometimes hard to hear the difference between words such as *you* and *you'll*, or *I* and *I'll*. It's also sometimes hard to hear the difference between *won't* and *want*. The rules for conditionals will help you figure out what you hear.

8.6 **A** **Listen and circle the words you hear.**

1 If you ***want to go / won't go*** to the grocery store, ***you / you'll*** need to bring a bag.
2 ***I lend / I'll lend*** you my raincoat if you ***want to borrow / won't borrow*** it.
3 If ***you / you'll*** like gadgets, ***you / you'll*** love this.
4 ***You learn / You'll earn*** a lot more if ***you / you'll*** listen carefully.

8.6 **B** **Listen again and repeat the sentences.**

C SPEAK **Work in pairs. Imagine you are going to lend your partner a gadget tonight. Follow the instructions.**

1 If you have a gadget with you (e.g. a phone, a smartwatch), show your partner what to do. Ask questions about your partner's gadget.
2 If you don't have a gadget, use an everyday object (e.g. a pen, your car keys) and pretend it's a gadget. Invent some cool functions for it.

SPEAKING

A **You are going to invent a new gadget and then promote it to the class. Use the ideas below and your own ideas to invent a gadget.**

What is it?	What's innovative about it?
a book, a chair, a food bowl, a hat, swimming goggles, a mirror, a light bulb, a plastic bottle, a puzzle, shoes, a toy, a TV, an umbrella	It can fly/talk/move by itself. It's connected to the internet. It contains a GPS device / a camera. It's for pets/birds/fish. It's very big/small.

B PLAN **Work in groups. Choose the best idea for your group's gadget and answer the questions:**

- What is special about your gadget?
- What problem does it solve?
- What else can you use to help you promote your gadget (e.g. pictures, stories)?
- What questions might people ask about your gadget?

C PRESENT **Promote your gadget to the class. At the end of each presentation, ask questions about other groups' gadgets.**

D REFLECT **Take a class vote to find out the most popular gadget. Would you like to buy the other groups' gadgets? Why/Why not? Do you think your gadgets could become real products?**

READING

A SPEAK Work in pairs. Look at the picture and answer the questions.

1 What do you think the people are doing? Why?

2 Have you ever done something similar? Why/Why not?

B PREDICT Work in pairs. Before you read *If you really can't wait …*, look at the five topic sentences (a–e) and discuss the questions. Use the strategies in the box to help you.

Topic sentences

The topic sentence is usually the first or second sentence in a paragraph. It tells you what the whole paragraph will be about.

You can usually understand a lot about a text just by reading and thinking about the topic sentences.

You can also use them to make predictions before reading the whole text to check.

a Marketers have a name for people who buy new gadgets before everyone else: innovators.

Why do you think marketers have a special name for these people? Why are marketers interested in them?

b A little further back in the line, I meet some fans who aren't just there to buy a phone.

Why do you think these fans are in the line?

c Near the back of the line, some people are feeling less positive.

Why do you think they're feeling less positive?

d It's five o'clock in the morning, and there are already over 200 people in the line outside the phone store.

Why do you think they're there so early in the morning?

e I decided to speak to some people in the line outside the phone store to find out … and I got a few surprises.

What surprises do you think the writer got?

If you really *can't wait …*

1 ___ It's cold and dark, but the people seem happy. In a few hours, the doors will open and they'll finally get their hands on the gadget of their dreams: a gorgeous new cell phone. Of course, if you don't want to stand in line all night, you can come to the store this afternoon when the lines will be gone. Even better, if you can wait six months or so, the same phone will cost half the price. But if you really need that phone right now, come and join the back of the line.

2 ___ I've always thought that was a terrible name – innovation normally means doing something extremely smart, like inventing a new machine. But what's innovative about buying expensive gadgets just because they're new? Of course, marketers love 'innovators' for two reasons: innovators are happy to spend a lot of money and they persuade the rest of us to buy those gadgets a few months later.

So why do they do it? 3 ___ The biggest surprise was that the people at the front of the line were actually being paid to be there. 'I work for a gadget store, Gary's Gadgets. My boss, Gary, is paying me,' said Bob, who is right at the front of the line. 'It's good for business because when the doors open, I'll be on TV around the world – wearing a T-shirt with the Gary's Gadgets logo.' Janice and Damian, who are second and third in the line, are also there for the money. 'We came here ten days ago, just to make sure we were first,' says Janice. 'But then Bob offered us $2500 to move ahead of us.'

4 ___ 'For me, it's a social event,' says a man named Mo. 'It's a great way to meet people who share my love of gadgets. I've had some amazing conversations in this line. Many of us come every year, so it feels like meeting old friends.' A woman named Ruby agrees, 'It's like going to a pop concert or a live sports game. I love the feeling of being at an important place at an important time.'

5 ___ 'I'm only here because of the special offer: 25 percent off for the first 200 customers,' explains a stressed-looking young woman named Lucy, 'so I'll be really annoyed if I'm number 201!' Her best friend, Fiona, looks annoyed already. 'I'm only here to keep Lucy company,' she says. 'I actually think it's a waste of time and money. I've been here all night and I'm really cold. I mean, this new phone looks exactly the same as last year's!' But Lucy looks shocked. 'There's only one difference that counts: the difference between the best … and second best.'

C READ FOR GIST Read the article. Match the topic sentences (a–e) with the paragraphs (1–5).

D READ FOR DETAIL Read again. Write *B* (Bob), *J* (Janice), *M* (Mo), *R* (Ruby), *L* (Lucy) or *F* (Fiona).

Which person …

1 has met people from the line at events like this before? M
2 paid to be at the front of the line? ___
3 doesn't want to buy a phone at all? ___
4 compares the experience to other exciting events? ___
5 arrived before anyone else? ___
6 enjoys talking to other people about gadgets? ___
7 is hoping to save some money? ___

E SPEAK Work in groups. Do you think it is right to call people who buy the latest gadgets *innovators*? Why/Why not?

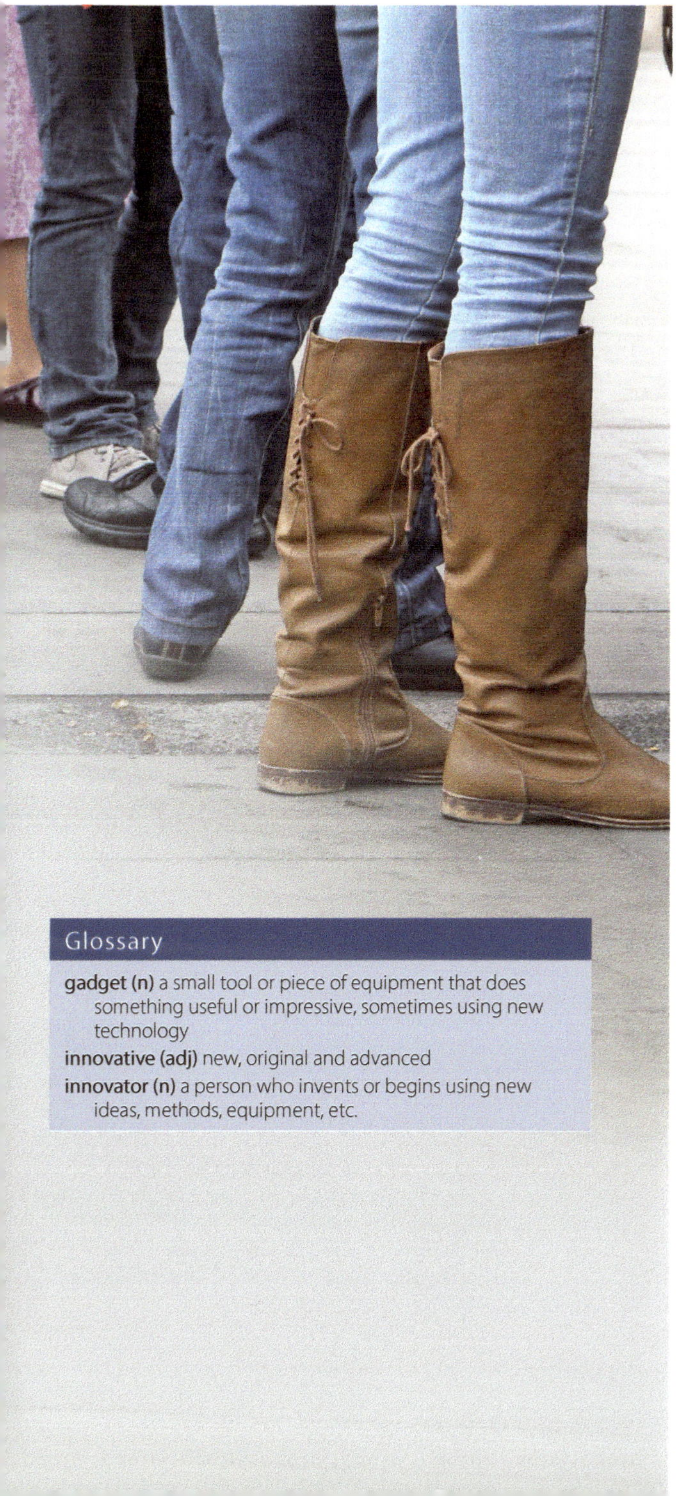

Glossary

gadget (n) a small tool or piece of equipment that does something useful or impressive, sometimes using new technology
innovative (adj) new, original and advanced
innovator (n) a person who invents or begins using new ideas, methods, equipment, etc.

GRAMMAR

Conditionals with modals and imperatives

A WORK IT OUT Read the rules. Then look at paragraph 1 of *If you really can't wait …* again and complete the examples.

Conditionals with modals and imperatives

Zero conditionals and first conditionals are very common. They can be very varied. Many patterns are possible.

For example, we can use imperatives in the result clause:

If you really need that phone right now, [1] ______________ *the back of the line.*

We can use modal verbs (e.g. *should, might, can, must*) in the *if*-clause or the result clause:

If you don't want to stand in line all night, you [2] ______________ *to the store this afternoon.*

If you [3] ______________ *six months or so, the same phone will cost half the price.*

B Go to the Grammar Hub on page X.

C SPEAK Work in pairs. Write five pieces of advice for people who are thinking of standing in line for the latest cell phone. Use these ideas and your own ideas:

- If you want to be at the front of the line, you should …
- If you can't afford a new phone right now, …
- If somebody offers you $2500 for your place in the line, …

SPEAKING HUB

A Work in pairs. Choose a gadget you both know well (e.g. phone, camera, laptop, webcam). You are going to give some advice to a friend who wants to buy one of these gadgets. Write notes on:

- price (simple version / best version?)
- features (what must/should it have?)
- risks (what might go wrong with it?)

B SPEAK Work in new pairs. Take turns role-playing the conversation. Student A is the friend who needs advice. Student B gives advice.

A: I don't know anything about photography. Do you have any recommendations for a new camera?
B: Well, it does really depend on how much you want to spend …

C DISCUSS What was the best advice you received? Would you buy the gadget your partner recommended?

Use positive language to promote a new product

Give a friend advice about choosing a gadget

Café Hub

8.3 Flat-packed

F give and follow instructions P sentence stress

COMPREHENSION

A Work in pairs and discuss the questions.

- Have you ever tried to build a piece of furniture or put up a shelf?
- How would you describe the experience – successful, frustrating, etc?
- Are you good at giving and following instructions?

B Match the words in the box with the tools in the pictures (a–d). Which tools do you think Sam and Zac will need to build a shelf?

allen key drill hammer helmet
pliers screwdriver spanner tape measure

a

b

c

d

C 00:00–02:53 Watch the first part of the video. How many tools do they use?

D 00:00–02:53 Put the instructions in the correct order (1–5). Watch the first part again and check your answers.

___ Lay out all the pieces in a row.
___ Insert the screws on both sides.
___ Put the screws into the correct holes.
___ Take the packet of screws.
___ Organize all of the pieces into the correct order.

E 02:54–04:13 How is Sam feeling and why? Watch the second part of the video to check your ideas.

FUNCTIONAL LANGUAGE

Giving and following instructions

A 02:54–04:13 Complete the phrases with the words in the box. Then watch the second part of the video again to check your answers.

after again correct do how let sure that thing

Sequencing

1 The first ____________ to do is …
2 When you've done ____________ …
3 ____________ that, you …

Explaining

4 Make ____________ you …
5 ____________ me show you …
6 This is how you ____________ it.

Checking

7 Sorry, can you say that ____________.
8 Is this ____________ you do it?
9 Are you sure this is ____________?

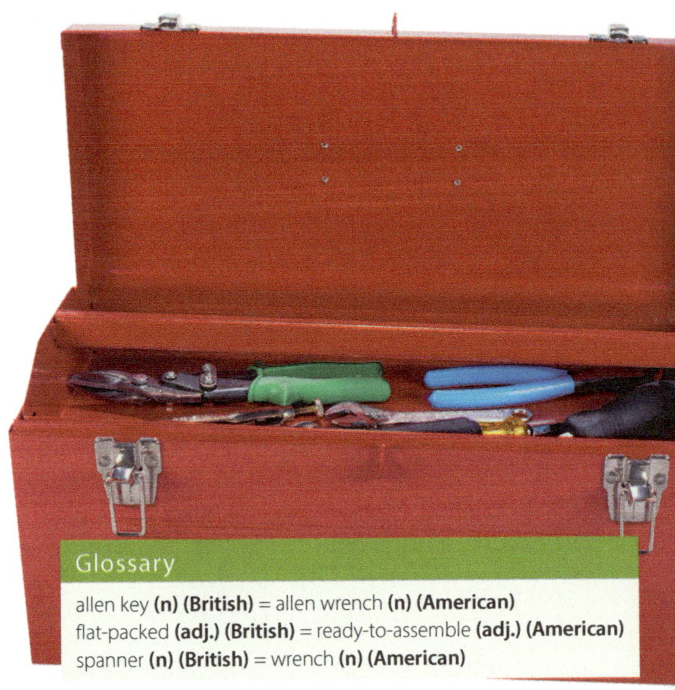

Glossary

allen key **(n) (British)** = allen wrench **(n) (American)**
flat-packed **(adj.) (British)** = ready-to-assemble **(adj.) (American)**
spanner **(n) (British)** = wrench **(n) (American)**

MILLY

SAM

NEENA

ZAC

GABY

B Work in pairs. Cover the functional language in Exercise A, and add sequencing phrases to the instructions in Comprehension Exercise D.

1 *The first thing to do is to organize all of the pieces into the correct order.*
2 ______
3 ______
4 ______
5 ______

USEFUL PHRASES

A Who says it? *Sam*, *Zac* or *Gaby*?

1 I know when something's wrong with you. ______
2 It's complicated. ______
3 She's been acting strangely around me. ______
4 A bit cold and unfriendly. ______
5 Whatever! ______

B How would you describe how each person feels in Exercise A? Choose the most appropriate adjective for each phrase.

concerned confused puzzled uninterested upset

C How do you say these useful phrases in your language?

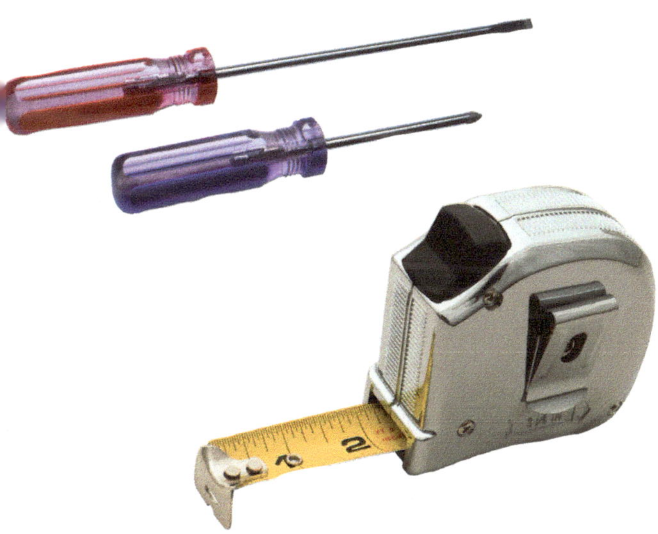

PRONUNCIATION
Sentence stress

8.7 **A** Underline the stressed words in the sentences (1–7). Then listen and check.

1 The first thing to do is to organize all of the pieces into the correct order.
2 Sorry, can you say that again?
3 What did you say?
4 When you've done that, take the packet of screws.
5 After that, you put the screws into the correct holes.
6 Is this how you do it?
7 Are you sure this is correct?

B Work in pairs. Practice saying the instructions in Exercise A, paying attention to the sentence stress.

SPEAKING

Work in pairs. Student A – go to the Communication Hub on page XX. Student B – go to the Communication Hub on page XXII. Follow the instructions.

Give and follow instructions

➤ Turn to page XXVI to learn how to write a biography.

Unit 8 Review

GRAMMAR

A Complete the dialogue with the adjective clauses in the box.

when which who

A: Hey, I like your watch. Is it new?

B: Yeah, I bought it last week [1] ________________ I was in Boston. It has a built-in phone and a button [2] ________________ you press to connect to the internet.

A: Cool. So what's the time?

B: Uh … I don't know. It worked for the man [3] ________________ sold it to me, but when I took it home, it didn't work at all.

B Choose the correct words to complete the article.

The liter of light

If [1]***you want / you'll want*** to make a difference in people's lives, a good, simple idea is best. Brazilian engineer Alfredo Moser noticed that many people in his country live in houses with no electricity. Of course, if [2]***there'll be / there's*** no electricity, the houses are usually very dark. It's hard for people to read or study at home [3]***if / unless*** they have enough light. Alfredo's solution? Cut a hole in your roof and put a plastic water bottle through the hole. If [4]***you do / you'll do*** it properly, the light will fill your house.

C Match the beginnings of the sentences (1–5) with the endings (a–e).

1 If you can't think of any good ideas,
2 If you must have the new phone today,
3 If you wear your smartwatch in the bathtub,
4 You shouldn't watch TV all the time
5 Don't worry

a if you're late – I'll wait for you.
b it might stop working properly.
c if you want to be more creative.
d join the line outside the store.
e go for a long walk.

VOCABULARY

A Complete the sentences with the correct form of the words in parentheses.

1 My old website looked horrible, so I asked my sister to ________________ (*designer*) a new one for me.
2 A great ________________ (*produce*) is one that makes a difference.
3 This machine's broken again! Can you call an ________________ (*engineering*) to come and fix it?
4 We've tried really hard, but we haven't had much ________________ (*succeed*) yet.
5 You just copied all my ideas! That isn't very ________________ (*innovate*), is it?

B Complete the advice with one word in each space.

Do you find it hard to come up [1] ______________ new ideas? Try these techniques to boost your creativity!

- If your mind goes [2] ________________, you probably need to take a break.
- Too much TV can block your creativity. Try to [3] ________________ completely.
- Try to relax and [4] ________________ your mind wander freely.
- Don't follow rules that don't exist! Learn to think outside the [5] ________________!
- Talk to a friend. This will help you to look at your problems [6] ________________ the outside.

C Complete the sentences with the best adjectives from the box.

gorgeous impressive sensible sophisticated suitable unique

1 Each user has a ________________ username and password – it can't be the same as anybody else's.
2 **A:** 'I built a laptop computer in my garage when I was ten years old.'
B: 'Wow! That's ________________!'
3 This camera isn't really ________________ for taking underwater pictures. If water gets into the electronics, it might break.
4 The best thing about my watch is that it looks ________________. Isn't it beautiful!
5 You can buy a simple microphone in the grocery store, but if you need something more ________________, with lots more options, you need to go to a specialist store.
6 It's fine to use another person's computer, but you need to be ________________. For example, don't use it to check your bank account.

FUNCTIONAL LANGUAGE

Correct the mistake in each part of the dialogue.

1 **A:** OK, here are the instructions for the table. Let's build this! The first thing do is take everything out of the box.
2 **B:** After that, put the legs on. Careful don't to lose the screws.
3 **A:** This is how you do it?
4 **B:** No, no, no! Those are the wrong screws. Let show you how to do it.
5 **A:** Are you sure this correct is? It looks wrong! Give me the instructions.

9 THE ARTS

> Art is unquestionably one of the purest and highest elements in human happiness.
>
> John Lubbock

A young man comes face to face with nature in a London gallery.

OBJECTIVES

- suggest improvements to a proposal
- plan an arts event
- report a conversation
- create a collaborative story
- talk about movies and books
- write a review

Work with a partner. Discuss the questions.

1 Look at the picture. Do you think this is art?

2 Look at the quote. Do you agree? Why/Why not?

3 Which of the arts do you like? What do you not like? Why? Are the arts important? Why/Why not?

9.1 Art for everybody

- Suggest improvements to a proposal
- Plan an arts event

V the arts; verbal idioms G second conditional P /tʃ/, /ʃ/ and /k/
S using linking words to understand the writer's opinion

A NEW ARTS VENUE FOR THE CITY CENTER

After the recent closure of a furniture factory in the city center, the city council has become the owner of a large warehouse. Council members voted last week to turn the warehouse into a major public arts venue. There will be a competition to choose the best use of the space. Please visit the council website for information on how to submit a proposal.
The warehouse consists of a large empty hall (120 m x 150 m), with offices upstairs.

LISTENING

A Look at the picture and read the article above. What would you like to use the warehouse for?

9.1 **B LISTEN FOR GIST** Listen to the three finalists from the competition speaking at a council meeting. Match the finalists (1–3) with the pictures (a–c).

1 Leon MacGregor ___ 3 Florian Quirk ___
2 Violet Spring ___

9.1 **C LISTEN FOR DETAIL** Listen again. Choose the correct answers.

1 Who does Leon mostly want to help?
   a people who don't work now
   b professional musicians
   c people who go out frequently
2 What exactly is Leon's dream?
   a to teach people to play musical instruments
   b to bring people together to learn new skills
   c to make money by selling tickets to concerts
3 Why do people travel to other cities to visit the theater?
   a because they are open every day
   b because there's no theater in their own city
   c because they don't want to spend their money at the Grand Theater
4 What is special about immersive theater?
   a The audience is on the stage with the actors.
   b Tickets are a lot more expensive than for other plays.
   c The audience doesn't just watch the play.
5 Why does Florian think art is important?
   a It makes money that can be spent on roads and schools.
   b It helps you to understand new ideas.
   c It helps you to relax when you're stressed.
6 How will Florian's idea help the people of the city?
   a It will give them a place to perform.
   b It will help the city's artists to sell their paintings.
   c It will make them think in a different way.

D SPEAK Work in pairs. Which proposal sounds the most interesting? Explain why.

a

b

c

VOCABULARY

The arts

A Complete the table with the words in the box. Some words can go in more than one place.

~~an audience~~ a choir a display an exhibit a gallery an instrument a live concert a musician an orchestra to perform live a performance a recording studio a rehearsal room to rehearse a scene a spectator a stage

Theater	Art (e.g. paintings)	Music
an audience		an audience

B What other words can you add to each group? Think about people and places connected with each topic.

C SPEAK Work in pairs and ask and answer the questions.

1 Do you ever rehearse what you are going to say before you say it? Think of examples.

2 Do you prefer to be a performer on a stage or a member of the audience? Why?

3 Can you play any musical instruments? Would you like to?

GRAMMAR

Second conditional

A WORK IT OUT Work in pairs. Look at the sentences (a–d) from the council meeting and discuss the questions (1–3).

a If we open a community music center, it will change thousands of people's lives.

b If we turned the warehouse into a theater, it would make a lot of money.

c If we had a good, modern theater in this city, it would be extremely popular.

d If the city council had three warehouses, maybe we could do all of those wonderful things.

1 Sentences **a** and **b** are both about the future. Which speaker is more certain that their plans will really happen?

2 In sentence **c**, does the city have a theater right now?

3 In sentence **d**, does the city council have three warehouses? Can they do all three things?

B Complete the rules with the words in the box.

could base past unreal were

Second conditional

1 Conditional sentences usually have two clauses: the *if*-clause and the result clause. To make second conditional sentences, we use *If* + simple ____________ and *would* + ____________ form of the verb.

2 With the verb *be*, we use ____________ instead of *was*.

If I were you, I'd vote for the first proposal.

3 We use the second conditional to talk about ____________ or impossible situations in the present or future.

4 If we are not sure of the result, we can use *might* or ____________ instead of *would* in the result clause.

C Go to the Grammar Hub on page XII.

D SPEAK Work in pairs and discuss the questions.

1 How would you feel if somebody asked you to sing in public?

2 If you were a successful musician, what sort of music would you play?

SPEAKING

A Work in pairs. Student A – read the box below. Student B – go to the Communication Hub on page XXI. Student C – go to the Communication Hub on page XXII. Read about one of the proposals for the Warehouse Project. Write about the advantages and disadvantages.

Proposal 1: Community music center

Costs (= money going out)		Income (= money coming in)
Building work: $450,000	Employees: $50,000/year	None – everything will be free for community groups
Equipment: $350,000	Other costs (e.g. electricity): $100,000/year	

- The community music center will save money by only opening for a few hours each day.
- Rehearsals/Workshops: Mondays, Wednesdays and Fridays, 10 am to 3 pm
- Concerts: Tuesdays and Thursdays, 12 pm to 2 pm
- Evenings and weekends: closed

B Tell your partner about your proposal. Then discuss what you like about each one. Suggest some improvements.

C Decide which proposal should win the competition. Why? Then share your ideas with the class.

READING

A SPEAK Work in pairs. Imagine you are watching a traditional play. What would you do if a character on the stage spoke to you? Would you be happy or would you feel uncomfortable?

B READ FOR MAIN IDEA Read the first paragraph of *The best (and the worst) of immersive theater*. Why has the writer written the article?

C READ FOR GIST Read the rest of the article. Match the recommendations (a–g) with the sections (1–6). There is one extra recommendation.

a Keep it simple.
b Tell a story.
c Make the audience feel special.
d Make it an experience for all the senses.
e Keep ticket prices as low as possible.
f Keep the rest of the audience out of sight.
g Make good use of the space.

The best (and the worst) of **immersive theater**

For most people, going to the theater is a chance to relax and let the actors do all the work. But in recent years, a new type of theater has appeared where the audience takes part in the play! When it works well, immersive theater can be breathtaking. But when it goes wrong, it can be awful. Here are my six recommendations based on my favorite (and least favorite!) immersive plays.

1 ___

Sometimes the building itself is part of the experience. A good example is *Hotel Impossible*, which took place in a real hotel building. Similarly, *The Dark Tunnels* took place inside real tunnels, which created a very scary atmosphere. However, a great location isn't everything. *Dangerous Heart* was in a beautiful palace, but the play didn't really take advantage of the space.

2 ___

In *Step by Step*, the audience was limited to 15, so we could interact one-on-one with the characters. During the play, the audience had to solve a crime, so we really had to pay attention to what we saw and heard. By the end, I was terrified and exhausted, but it was an unforgettable experience.

3 ___

Some immersive plays feel far too complicated, with too many characters and storylines. For example, *Yellow and Blue* had amazing special effects, but I couldn't keep track of who was who. In *The Quiet Visitors*, however, there were only six characters in a large empty room. We had to use our imaginations, and the effect was incredibly powerful.

4 ___

The worst thing about immersive theater? Other members of the audience! The play *Life with the Lions* got rid of this problem by making the audience wear animal costumes. I felt silly in my zebra costume, but at least we couldn't tell the difference between actors and spectators. In *The Dark Tunnels*, we all wore black clothes and masks so the members of the audience were almost invisible to each other.

5 ___

Without a strong story, immersive theater can easily fall flat – it feels like something's missing. In *Hotel Impossible*, for example, lots of interesting things happened, but the whole play didn't really go anywhere. In *The Quiet Visitors*, however, there was a clear beginning, a middle … and a shocking surprise at the end.

6 ___

It isn't just about what the audience sees and hears. The best immersive plays make use of the senses of taste, smell and touch, too. In *Dangerous Heart*, we enjoyed a delicious meal as part of the experience. Similarly, in *The Dark Tunnels*, the unpleasant underground smell added to the sense of danger. And in *The Quiet Visitors*, when the room suddenly went as cold as ice, the effect was terrifying.

D Look at the highlighted words in the article. What is the writer's opinion? Use the strategies in the box to help you. Choose + (positive) or – (negative).

Using linking words to understand the writer's opinion

When you're trying to figure out the writer's opinion, don't just look for positive words (e.g. *amazing*, *interesting*) and negative words (e.g. *unpleasant*, *terrifying*).

Writers regularly use words like *for example*, *similarly* and *however* to link their opinions to earlier sentences.

1 the location for *The Dark Tunnels* + / –
2 the characters and story in *Yellow and Blue* + / –
3 the characters and story in *The Quiet Visitors* + / –
4 the story in *Hotel Impossible* + / –
5 the experience for the senses in *The Dark Tunnels* + / –
6 the experience for the senses in *The Quiet Visitors* + / –

E SPEAK Work in pairs. Which of the plays from the article would you most like to see? Which would you least like to see? Why? Tell your partner.

VOCABULARY
Verbal idioms

Verbal idioms

Verbal idioms are fixed phrases that work as verbs with a single meaning.

A Go to the Vocabulary Hub on page XVIII.

B SPEAK Complete the sentences so they are true for you. Then work in pairs and tell your partner what happened.

1 I had an opportunity to … but I didn't take advantage of it, because …
2 Everything went wrong when I …
3 I'm planning to get rid of …
4 I once tried to (tell a joke/story, etc.), but it fell flat, because …

PRONUNCIATION
/ʧ/, /ʃ/ and /k/

9.2 **A** How do you pronounce *ch* in these words? Listen and repeat.

character charge chef choice choir orchestra

ch

ch is usually pronounced /ʧ/ (as in *cheese*). But there are also a few words where *ch* is pronounced /ʃ/ (as in *mustache*) or /k/ (as in *chemist*).

B Find and underline *ch* in these sentences. Then write /ʧ/, /ʃ/ or /k/ above each example.

1 My children didn't go to school today – they both had bad stomachaches. (/ʧ/ above *ch* in *children*)
2 If I were a mechanic, I might be able to fix this machine, but I don't know anything about technology.
3 My sister is a chemist; she's doing some research into new techniques for recycling harmful chemicals.

9.3 **C** Listen and check.

D SPEAK Work in pairs. Practice saying the sentences. Listen and check your partner's pronunciation.

SPEAKING HUB

A Work in groups. Discuss ideas for an immersive theater performance. Think about:

- story: Will you use an existing story or create your own?
- location: Where will it take place? How could you make use of the location?
- interactivity: How will the actors interact with the audience?

B PLAN Choose your best idea and add more details. Follow the advice in *The best (and the worst) of immersive theater* on page 100.

C PRESENT Present your idea to the class.

D REFLECT Which immersive play would you most like to watch? Why?

- Suggest improvements to a proposal
- Plan an arts event

9.2 Tell me a story

- Report a conversation
- Create a collaborative story

G – reported speech **V** – reporting verbs **P** – using your voice to make a story more interesting
S – listening for definitions of new words

Francis Scott Key Fitzgerald (1896–1940) was one of the most important American writers of the 20th century. His best-known novel, *The Great Gatsby* (1925), is an American classic. It paints a powerful portrait of life in 1920s America, a period known as the Jazz Age. For many young people in America, this was a time for partying and having fun, with new types of music, new ways of dancing and new fashions.

READING

A Work in pairs. Read about F. Scott Fitzgerald and look at the pictures. Have you read *The Great Gatsby*? Why do you think it is 'an American classic'?

I haven't read the book but I have seen the movie starring Leonardo DiCaprio.

9.4 **B** Listen to a conversation between two friends, Joe and Nadia. Answer the questions.

1 Who is Jay Gatsby?
2 Why doesn't Joe want to borrow the book? Why does he change his mind?
3 Why does Nadia like the book?

CHAPTER 3: I MEET GATSBY

PART 1

One day, I was invited to one of Gatsby's parties. As soon as I arrived, I began to look for Gatsby to thank him for his invitation. But no one knew where he was.

As I went to get a drink, I saw Jordan Baker. I walked toward her, glad to see someone I knew.

'I thought you might be here,' Jordan said.

We took our drinks and sat down at a small table under a tree. Jordan began to talk to a girl in a yellow dress.

'Do you come to these parties often?' Jordan asked her.

'I come when I can,' the girl said. 'No one cares what I do, so I always have a good time. Last time I was here, I tore my dress. Do you know, Gatsby sent me a new one! It cost him 265 dollars!'

PART 2

Supper was now being served. Jordan and I left our table and went to look for Gatsby.

People were dancing now. The voices and the laughter were very loud. The moon was high in the sky.

Jordan and I sat down at a table with a well-dressed man of my own age. I was enjoying myself, now. The music stopped for a moment. The man at our table looked at me and smiled.

'I think I know your face,' the man said. 'Weren't you in France during the War?'

'Yes, I was.'

'Me, too,' he said. We talked about the War for a few minutes. Then the man told me that **he had a new motorboat.**

'Want to go out with me in the morning, old sport?' he asked.

'Sure, what time?'

'Let's say nine o'clock.'

I looked at the yard and smiled.

'This is an unusual party,' I told the man. 'I haven't seen my host yet. Gatsby sent me an invitation this morning. I ought to thank him.'

The man stared at me in surprise.

'I'm Gatsby,' he said. 'I thought you knew, old sport. I'm not a very good host, am I?'

Gatsby smiled. He had a pleasant smile. His smile made me feel important. I looked at Gatsby with interest. He was a tough-looking young man, but he had beautiful clothes and beautiful manners.

PART 3

A few guests were standing near Gatsby. I went up to him to say goodbye.

'Don't forget we're going out in the boat, old sport,' he said. 'At nine o'clock.'

Gatsby smiled at me.

'Goodnight, old sport, goodnight.'

I walked across the lawn in the moonlight. The cars drove away. The yard was quiet and empty.

All alone, Gatsby stood on the white steps, waving goodbye.

Glossary

old sport (phrase) a popular way of saying 'my friend' in the 1920s

C READ FOR DETAIL Read *The Great Gatsby*, Chapter 3, Part 1. Are the sentences true (T) or false (F)? Correct the false sentences.

1 Gatsby invited Nick Carraway (the storyteller) to his party. ___
2 Nick already knew most of the people at the party. ___
3 Jordan was surprised to see Nick. ___
4 Gatsby is very careful with his money. ___

D Read Part 2. What do we learn about Gatsby? Write notes on:

1 his appearance (= his clothes and the way he looks).
2 his manners (= the way he treats other people).
3 his background (= what he has done in the past).

E Read Part 3. Why do you think Gatsby has so many parties?

GRAMMAR

Reported speech

A WORK IT OUT Look at the phrase in bold from *The Great Gatsby*, Chapter 3, Part 2. What do you think Gatsby actually said?

Direct speech: 'I ____________ a new motorboat.'

B Complete the examples in the correct tense.

Direct speech	Reported speech
Simple present 'My name's Jay Gatsby.'	**Simple past** He told me his name [1] ____________ Jay Gatsby.
Present progressive 'I'm really enjoying the party.'	**Past progressive** I told him I [2] ____________ really enjoying the party.
Present perfect 'I've never met Gatsby.'	**Past perfect** He said he [3] ____________ never met Gatsby.
Simple past 'Gatsby sent me a new dress.'	**Past perfect** She said Gatsby [4] ____________ sent her a new dress.
can 'I can't see the host.'	*could* I told him I [5] ____________ see the host.
will 'We'll have a great time on my boat.'	*would* He said we [6] ____________ have a great time on his boat.

C Go to the Grammar Hub on page XII.

D Report the sentences (1–5) from *The Great Gatsby*.

1 'Do you come to these parties often?' Jordan asked her.
Jordan asked the girl if she came to these parties often.

2 'I come when I can,' the girl said.
____
____

3 'I think I know your face,' the man said.
____
____

4 'This is an unusual party,' I told the man. 'I haven't seen my host yet.'
____
____

5 'Gatsby sent me an invitation this morning.'
____
____

E SPEAK Work in pairs. Use your imagination to tell the next part of the story. Report the conversation between Jay and Nick the next morning.

SPEAKING

A Think about the questions below. Write notes.

1 Do you read a lot of novels? What sort of books do you enjoy? Which books would you recommend? Why?
2 Do you ever read books in English? What have you read? Did you find it easy or difficult? Do you need to understand every word or can you simply relax and enjoy the story?

B Work in pairs. Ask and answer the questions from Exercise A. Ask follow-up questions and give examples.

C Work with a new partner. Tell your new partner about your conversation.

LISTENING

A SPEAK Work in groups and discuss the questions.

1 What are some situations where people tell each other stories?

2 Are stories just for fun, or do they have a serious purpose?

3 Do you like telling stories? What kind of stories?

4 What skills do you need to tell great stories? When was the last time you told a story?

- Where were you?
- Who did you tell it to?
- Why did you tell it?
- What was the story about?

9.5 **B LISTEN FOR GIST** Listen to the conversation between two friends, Zoe and Jacob. They are talking about storytelling. Put the pictures (a–c) in the order that they discuss them (1–3).

1 ___ 2 ___ 3 ___

Glossary

dice (n) a small block of wood or plastic with six sides marked with spots that you roll or throw to play a game

end up (with) (phrasal verb) to be in a particular place or state after doing something or because of doing it

a

b

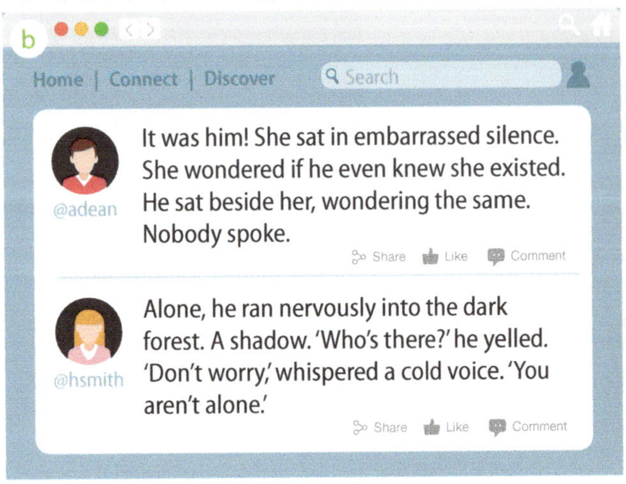

9.5 **C LISTEN FOR KEY WORDS** Listen again and complete the definitions of the new words. Use the strategies in the box to help you.

Listening for definitions of new words

Speakers usually pause before and after an important new word. They usually place extra stress on the word itself.

When you hear an important new word, listen carefully for a definition or explanation.

1 Flash fiction: A story with a word limit, usually ________________ words.

2 Micro-stories: These are stories on social ________________ sites (e.g. Twitter). A whole story told in a ________________-character message.

3 A twist: When something happens in the story that you didn't ________________.

4 Collaborative stories: Stories that are created by a large group of people working ________________.

5 Pass the paper: You write one line of a ________________ on a sheet of paper, fold it down and pass it to the next player, who writes the next ________________, and so on.

6 Add a word: You sit in a ________________. The first person says the first ________________ from a sentence, and then the next person says the next word.

7 Story dice: A set of ________________ dice, and each one has six ________________, one on each side.

D SPEAK Work in groups. Play *Add a word*.

E DISCUSS Work in groups and discuss the questions.

1 Have you ever played any of the games or tried any of the story techniques mentioned in the conversation? Would you like to?

2 Do you think word limits make it easier or harder to write a good story?

3 Do you prefer working collaboratively or by yourself?

c

VOCABULARY

Reporting verbs

A Look at the examples of micro-stories in Listening Exercise B, picture b. Which verbs are used instead of *say* and *think*? Why?

B Look at the information in the box. Use a dictionary to check any new verbs.

Reporting verbs

Instead of using *say* and *tell*, we can use more interesting and descriptive reporting verbs.

verb (+ *that*) + reported speech: *add, admit, agree, argue, explain, insist, mention, predict, promise, repeat, reply, say, yell, warn, whisper*

verb + somebody (+ *that*) + reported speech: *advise, persuade, promise, remind, tell, warn*

verb + reported question: *ask, explain, wonder*

verb + infinitive: *agree, ask, promise, refuse*

verb + somebody + infinitive: *advise, ask, persuade, promise, remind, tell, warn*

C Choose the best reporting verbs to complete the sentences from the conversation between Zoe and Jacob.

1 Zoe asked how Jacob's creative writing class was going, and he ***added / reminded / replied*** that it was going really well.

2 Zoe ***agreed / mentioned / wondered*** whether Jacob was joking about micro-stories.

3 Jacob ***persuaded / warned / whispered*** Zoe that it's usually better if the writer provides less information.

4 Zoe ***agreed / insisted / predicted*** that the second story was really powerful.

5 Zoe ***added / explained / persuaded*** how 'Pass the paper' works.

6 Zoe ***agreed / promised / yelled*** that Jacob would enjoy playing 'Pass the paper', but Jacob ***admitted / insisted / refused*** to play.

7 Jacob ***admitted / predicted / yelled*** that most of the stories are trash.

8 Zoe ***argued / explained / mentioned*** that she had been a student in California.

9 Jacob ***argued / predicted / reminded*** Zoe that the story could have up to 1,000 words.

10 Jacob ***insisted / warned / whispered*** Zoe that it wouldn't be easy to write the story.

PRONUNCIATION

Using your voice to make a story more interesting

9.6 **A** Listen again to Jacob reading the two micro-stories. How does he use his voice to make the stories sound more interesting? Think about:

- speaking quickly, slowly, loudly or quietly.
- showing emotions.
- pausing.

B SPEAK Work in pairs. Look at the audio script on page XXXII. Take turns reading the two stories aloud. Try to use your voice to make the stories sound more interesting.

C SPEAK Look at the story you wrote in Listening Exercise D. How can you use your voice to make it sound more interesting? Read your story to the class.

D REFLECT Work in groups. Which is the best story? Which storyteller used his/her voice most effectively?

SPEAKING HUB

A You are going to tell a story based on four pictures. Student A – go to the Communication Hub on page XIX. Student B – go to the Communication Hub on page XXI. Look at the pictures and spend one minute thinking about your story. Do not worry if your story is not very good yet!

B SPEAK Work in pairs. Take turns telling your story. While your partner is talking, listen carefully to his/her story. You can help if your partner runs out of ideas.

C PLAN Work together to improve your stories and make them longer. Can you join your two stories together into a single story? Use these ideas to help you:

- Who exactly were the people?
- What were the characters trying to do?
- How did they feel?
- What did they say?
- What happened next?

D PRESENT Share your stories with the class. Use your voice to make them as interesting as possible.

E REFLECT Work in groups. Which story did you like best? Why? Who was the best storyteller?

- Report a conversation
- Create a collaborative story

Café Hub

9.3 Leaving London

F– talk about movies and books P– words connected to movies

COMPREHENSION

A Work in pairs and discuss the questions.

- What kind of movies do you like and dislike?
- Do you ever cry at movies? When was the last time?
- Do you prefer reading a book or watching the movie based on the book?

B Think of a movie you have seen recently and answer the questions.

1 What kind of movie was it? Romantic comedy, horror, etc?

2 Who was in it?

3 What kind of ending did it have?

C ▶ 00:00–03:36 Watch the first part of the video and answer the questions in Exercise B. Why is Gaby so emotional?

D ▶ 03:36–05:03 Watch the second part of the video with the volume turned off. What do you think is happening? Discuss with a partner and then watch with the volume turned up and check your ideas.

FUNCTIONAL LANGUAGE

Talking about movies

▶ Match the two halves of phrases you can use to talk about movies. Watch the video again and check your ideas.

Talking about movies	
1 If you like sad and romantic films,	a sad ending.
2 It's got Jessica Brune in it.	b tearjerker.
3 It's a real	c where he writes the letter to her.
4 That was a really	d reading.
5 It's really worth	e amazing performance.
6 I thought the plot was good	f Oh really, she's a brilliant actor.
7 What an	g then this is the one for you.
8 I loved the scene	h and it felt like real life.

USEFUL PHRASES

A Match the useful phrases (1–6) with the phrases that have a similar meaning (a–f).

1 Yeah, right!	a There isn't always a happy ending.
2 Things don't always work out perfectly.	b I've almost done all my work.
3 There's something I've been meaning to tell you.	c We don't believe you.
4 We're going to miss you.	d I've been waiting for the right time to say this.
5 Do you want a hand?	e We don't want you to leave.
6 Just finishing up here.	f Can I help you?

B How do you say these useful phrases in your language?

Glossary

brilliant **(adj.) (British)** = great/fabulous/excellent **(adj.) (American)**
film/s **(n) (British)** = movie/s **(n) (American)**

MILLY

SAM

NEENA

ZAC

GABY

PRONUNCIATION

Words connected to movies

9.7 **A** These are some of the words connected to movies that appear in the video. Put them in the correct column according to the word stress. Listen and check your answers.

actor amazing brilliant comedy ending horror movie performance ~~review~~ romantic tearjerker terrible

oO	Oo	oOo	Ooo
review			

B Work in pairs. Complete the sentences so that they are true for you. Compare with your partner.

1 The most terrible movie I've ever seen was …
2 My favorite comedy is …
3 The most fabulous actor in my country is …
4 I'd give the Oscar for the most amazing performance to …
5 The best place to read movie reviews is …

SPEAKING

A Think of your favorite movie of all time and write notes.

1 What's the title of the movie?
2 What kind of movie is it?
3 Who stars in the movie?
4 What happens and how does it end?
5 What do you particularly like about the plot and characters?
6 How did the movie make you feel?

B DISCUSS Work in pairs. Take turns describing your favorite movie.

Talk about movies and books

➤ Turn to page XXVII to learn how to write a review.

Unit 9 Review

A Correct the four mistakes in the sentences.

1 I'd feel really strange if one of the actors start talking to me.

____

2 If I had a little more time, I'll come and watch the movie with you, but I'm much too busy.

____

3 If I'd know the answer, I'd tell you, but I don't so I can't.

____

4 You'd be a better actor if you can remember your lines!

____

B Change the direct speech into reported speech.

1 'My daughter is a talented artist.'
He said that ______________ a talented artist.

2 'Immersive theater is becoming a lot more popular all the time.'
She said that immersive theater ______________ a lot more popular all the time.

3 'Do you prefer reading books or watching movies?'
He asked me ______________ reading books or watching movies.

4 'I can't paint, but I can draw fairly well.'
She told me she ______________ fairly well.

5 'How much will the tickets cost?'
She asked me ______________.

6 'Be quiet! We're trying to rehearse!'
They told me ______________ because they ______________ to rehearse.

7 'Have you ever seen a famous band live in concert?'
He asked me ______________ a famous band live in concert.

VOCABULARY

A Complete the sentences with the words in the box.

choir display gallery orchestra scene spectators

Reviews

1 We went to an amazing classical music concert last week. The ______________ had over 50 musicians!

2 The play was very smart. There was an unexpected twist in the final ______________.

3 The Japanese Culture Week ended with a wonderful ______________ by a group of traditional dancers.

4 I'm a member of a ______________. There are 30 of us, and we practice singing three times a week.

5 I'm really excited. There's going to be an exhibit of my paintings at the local ______________!

6 It was such an amazing tennis game. The ______________ clapped for ten minutes!

B Read the conversation and choose the correct verb to complete the idioms.

A: So? What did you think of my short story?

B: Well, I thought it was a little too complicated. I couldn't [1]***stay / keep*** track of who was who.

A: Really? So do you think I should [2]***get / go*** rid of some of the main characters?

B: Yes, that would be much better. And some of your characters were too similar to each other. It needs to be much easier for the reader to [3]***tell / talk*** the difference between them.

A: OK, that's a good point. I'll try to [4]***hold / pay*** attention to things like that in future. Anything else?

B: The beginning was excellent, and I loved the fact that the whole story [5]***takes / starts*** place on a train, but then you didn't really [6]***do / make*** use of that idea later in the book. I think you should definitely try to [7]***take / make*** advantage of the train trip more.

A: OK. What did you think of the ending?

B: I thought the ending was fairly weak, so the story kind of [8]***falls / keeps*** flat at the end. But … apart from that, it was great.

C Match the beginnings of the sentences (1–7) with the endings (a–g).

1 'Shhh! Don't talk during the play,'
2 'You must keep your promise and come to watch the show,'
3 'The gallery might be fairly crowded tomorrow,'
4 'Don't forget to buy a ticket,'
5 'Yes, you're absolutely right,'
6 'I didn't write my story – I copied it from the internet,'
7 'Where is everybody?'

a she reminded him.
b he admitted.
c she predicted.
d he insisted.
e she wondered.
f he agreed.
g she whispered.

FUNCTIONAL LANGUAGE

Choose the correct words to complete the conversation.

A: I want to go to the movie theater tonight, but all the new movies look a little boring.

B: Really? What about *Silly Story 2*? I thought the lead actor, Max Connor, was great [1]***at / in / on / with*** it. If you like funny movies, it's definitely the movie [2]***by / for / of / to*** you.

A: Oh, yes, I saw the ad for it. But I didn't like *Silly Story 1*. The plot was really difficult to [3]***follow / mention / predict / record***, and it was very sad at the end.

B: Yeah, I know what you mean. But this one's much better, and it really [4]***had / did / made / took*** me laugh. And it has a really happy [5]***ending / finishing / starting / stopping***.

A: Don't tell me how it ends! You'll spoil it for me!

B: OK, sorry, but I think it's really [6]***worth / love / miss / recommend*** seeing. Definitely watch this movie.

10 PSYCHOLOGY

The purpose of psychology is to give us a completely different idea of the things we know best.

Paul Valéry

A hiker watches a storm approach in New South Wales, Australia.

OBJECTIVES

- talk about different versions of past events
- talk about past mistakes
- talk about your wishes and regrets
- plan a to-do list
- make and accept apologies
- write a report

Work with a partner. Discuss the questions.

1 Look at the picture. Where do you go when you want to think?

2 Look at the quote. Do you agree?

3 Work in pairs. Tell your partner what you do when you need to reflect on a problem.

10.1 Making up your mind

- Talk about different versions of past events
- Talk about past mistakes

V – psychology verbs; expressions with *mind*
P – third conditional
G – third conditional; *should have* + past participle
S – listening for phrases that support an argument

READING

A SPEAK Work in pairs. Go the **Communication Hub** on **page XXIII**.

B READ FOR MAIN IDEA Read *Do you think you think rationally? Think again!* What is the connection between the three sub-headings and pictures 1–3 above?

C READ FOR DETAIL Read again. Are the sentences true (T) or false (F)? Correct the false sentences.

1. New research has shown that we're good at making rational decisions. ___
2. After we've thought about a hook number, it's easy to think of a number that's a long way from that hook. ___
3. We would probably make better decisions if we ignored hook numbers. ___
4. If we were more rational, we would worry more about buried costs. ___
5. In the example about the weekend break, the money you've spent on the hotel and travel is a buried cost. ___
6. Filtering involves presenting a situation in a way that makes it sound better (or worse) than it really is. ___

D SPEAK Work in pairs. Can you think of any examples of hook numbers, buried costs or filtering from your own life? Tell your partner.

DO YOU THINK YOU THINK RATIONALLY? THINK AGAIN!

For centuries, psychologists assumed that people think rationally and make decisions based on facts. But we're actually much less rational than we think.

HOOK NUMBERS

Look again at the quiz. Question 1a is clearly nonsense: of course we have more than 70 thoughts per day! So it shouldn't affect our answers to question 1b. But for most people, the number 70 acts as a hook. It encourages us to think of a number that isn't too far from 70. But if the hook number had been much higher, say 70 million, it would have made us think of a number in the millions. And if we hadn't seen a hook at all, we might have chosen a more likely answer: around 70,000 thoughts per day.

Sales people use hook numbers to persuade us to spend much more than we should, for example, by tricking us into believing a watch must be worth thousands of dollars.

BURIED COSTS

A buried cost is time, money or effort that we've already spent and can't get back. It would be rational to ignore buried costs when making decisions; they're gone, so we should forget about them. But for most of us, waste feels like physical pain, and we usually spend even more time, money and effort trying to avoid that pain. Look back at question 2 in the quiz. The money you've spent is gone. Instead of regretting the past, we should forget it and focus on the future. When you're sick, you should stay home and get better.

VOCABULARY
Psychology verbs

A Match the beginnings of the definitions (1–8) with the endings (a–h). Use *Do you think you think rationally? Think again!* to help you.

1 If something **affects** or **influences** you,
2 If you **assume** that something is true,
3 If something **attracts** you,
4 If you **avoid** doing something,
5 If you **encourage** or **persuade** somebody to do something,
6 If you **regret** something,
7 If something **tempts** you,
8 If somebody **tricks** you into doing something,

a you say something that makes him/her want to do it.
b you feel bad about something you did (or didn't do) in the past.
c they make you do it by lying or hiding the truth.
d you believe it although you haven't checked for sure.
e you are careful not to do it.
f you want it, even though it might be bad for you.
g it changes the way you think or behave.
h you like it and want to have it.

B Choose the correct verbs to complete the questions.

1 How do marketers and advertisers ***avoid*** / ***tempt*** us to buy things we don't really want or need?
2 When you go shopping, which things ***attract*** / ***influence*** your decision to buy something? Is it possible that the stores use psychological tricks to affect your choices?

C SPEAK Work in pairs. Ask and answer the questions in Exercise B.

FILTERING

In question 3 from the quiz, were you tempted by School A? That 75 percent pass rate sounds great, doesn't it? What about School B, with all those failures? No, thanks! Of course, your rational side knows that School B is better – a 20 percent failure rate means there's an 80 percent pass rate. But we can't help being influenced by words like *pass* and *fail*.
We're strongly attracted to positive words like *success*, *save* and *free*. But negative words are even more powerful. We hate *losing*, *wasting* or *missing* things. So if you see an ad that warns, 'Don't miss your last chance to save,' remember that someone is trying to trick our irrational minds.

Glossary

bury (v) to put something in the ground and cover it with earth
filter (v) if you filter a photo, you change or improve the appearance of the image before posting it on social media
hook (n) a curved piece of metal or plastic fixed to a pole or with a handle at the other end, used for catching hold of something

GRAMMAR
Third conditional

A WORK IT OUT Work in pairs. Look at the sentence from *Do you think you think rationally? Think again!* Then choose the correct words to complete the rules.

If the hook number had been much higher, say 70 million, it would have made us think of a number in the millions.

Third conditional

1 We use the third conditional to talk about imaginary situations in ***the past*** / ***the present***.
2 Conditional sentences usually have ***two*** / ***three*** clauses: the ***if***-clause and the result clause. To make a third conditional sentence, we use:
if + past perfect, ***would*** + ***have*** + past participle
3 We ***can*** / ***can't*** use ***might*** or ***could*** instead of ***would*** in the result clause.

B Find and underline another third conditional sentence in the article.

C Go to the Grammar Hub on page XIV.

D SPEAK Work in pairs. Write three third conditional sentences that are true for you. Tell your partner about the situations in your sentences.

PRONUNCIATION
Third conditional

10.1 **A** Listen and repeat the third conditional sentence. What do you notice about the pronunciation of *had*, *would* and *have*?

If I'd thought about it more carefully, I'd have made a better decision.

B SPEAK Work in pairs. Practice saying the sentences you wrote in Grammar Exercise D. Listen and check your partner's pronunciation.

SPEAKING

Work in pairs and discuss the questions.

1 Think of a time in the past when you paid too much for something or bought something you didn't really want or need. What happened? Why? What would have happened if you'd thought more carefully?
When I bought my first car, I thought it was perfect. But I didn't check whether it actually worked properly! In the end, I spent a lot of money fixing it and sold it again. If I'd …

2 Think of a time in the past when you made a bad decision because you didn't have enough information or experience. What would you have done differently if you'd known then what you know now?
I received an email from my bank last week telling me to click on a link to change my password. Luckily, I noticed that the link was to a completely different site. But if I hadn't noticed …

LISTENING

A SPEAK Work in groups and discuss the questions.

1 Do you find shopping relaxing or stressful? Why?

2 When you're shopping for clothes and shoes, do you find it easy to decide what to buy?

10.2 **B LISTEN FOR MAIN IDEA** Listen to a conversation between two friends, Robert and Vicky. What do they say about the items in the pictures (a–d)?

Glossary

common sense (n) the ability to use good judgment and make sensible decisions

paradox (n) a statement consisting of two parts that seem to mean the opposite of each other

perfectionist (n) someone who always wants things to be done perfectly

10.2 **C** Listen again. How does Robert support his arguments? Use the strategies in the box to help you.

Listening for phrases that support an argument

Sometimes when you listen, you need to decide how strong a person's arguments are. Pay attention to the techniques they use to support their argument.

Common sense:

- *Surely, Of course, Obviously, Clearly, As you can imagine, …*

Facts and statistics:

- *In fact, …; The researchers found that …*

Examples and details:

- *For example, …; For instance, …*

Expert opinions:

- *According to Professor Schwartz …; He's shown that …*

10.2 **D LISTEN FOR DETAIL** Listen again. Complete the notes about the conversation.

1 **The Paradox of Choice:** According to Professor Barry Schwartz (an ___American___ psychologist), too many ___________ makes us ___________.

2 **Shampoo company:** Cut choices from ___________ to ___________. Sales went up by ___________ percent.

3 **Robert's experience of buying a laptop:** He went to a small store with ___________ laptops to choose from. Took ___________ minutes to choose and buy a laptop.

4 **Perfectionists regret their choices:** Vicky bought ___________ different pairs of shoes, but took each pair back to the store.

5 **Quick deciders don't worry about perfection:** When Robert finds jeans that are ___________ enough, he buys them and stops worrying. Only takes them back to store if they're ___________.

E SPEAK Work in groups and discuss the questions.

1 Have you ever experienced the Paradox of Choice? Think about the following situations:
   - shopping
   - choosing what to watch on TV or online
   - making important life decisions
   - cooking or eating

2 Are you a perfectionist or a quick decider? What about other people in your family?

3 How can stores, websites and other businesses help us deal with the Paradox of Choice?

GRAMMAR

should have + past participle

A WORK IT OUT Look at the sentences from the conversation between Vicky and Robert. Then choose the correct words to complete the rules.

So with your laptop, you **should have gone** to a smaller store.

I realized that they weren't perfect and I **shouldn't have bought** them.

> ***should have* + past participle**
>
> 1 We write ***should*** (***not***) + ***have*** + **past participle / base form**.
>
> 2 We use ***should have done*** to talk about mistakes that we ***make / made*** in the past and imagine how we could have avoided those mistakes.

B Go to the Grammar Hub on page XIV.

C SPEAK Work in pairs. Use *should/shouldn't have done* to talk about these situations.

1 Angela went shopping for a new coat. She found a great coat in the first store, but she went to ten more stores to make sure it was the best one. When she went back to buy it, somebody else had bought it.

2 Kasia bought a used computer five years ago, but it didn't work properly. Although she had enough money to buy a new one, she kept using the old one for years.

VOCABULARY

Expressions with *mind*

10.2 **A Complete the sentences (1–8) from the conversation with the expressions in the box. Then listen again and check your answers.**

> all in the mind   bear in mind   change my mind
> of two minds   made up my mind   never mind
> put your mind to   would you mind if

1 ______________________ I borrowed your laptop for a few minutes?

2 Just ______________________ that it's really slow.

3 I found two that I liked, but I was ______________________ and I couldn't decide which one to buy.

4 But ______________________. I still have my old computer, so it isn't so bad.

5 Once I've ______________________, I stick with my decision.

6 You think it's impossible, but maybe it's ______________________.

7 I think you can become a quick decider – you just need to ______________________ it!

8 But what if I ______________________ later?

B SPEAK Work in pairs. What do you think the expressions in Exercise A mean?

C SPEAK Work in pairs and discuss the questions.

1 Quick deciders are generally less stressed, but there are some dangers connected with making quick decisions. What should they **bear in mind** before making a decision?

2 How long does it usually take you to **make up your mind** about whether you can trust somebody? What might make you **change your mind** about them?

SPEAKING HUB

A Read the sentences about regrets. Do you agree or disagree with them? Why?

1 You should never regret anything. Your mistakes are part of who you are.

2 You should regret the things you haven't done more than the things you have done.

B Think about two or three mistakes you have made in the past. What did you do? What did you not do? What should or should you not have done?

C Work in pairs. Tell your partner about some of the mistakes you have made. While your partner is talking, listen carefully, and then ask questions to find out more information.

> **Finding out more information**
>
> Really? So what did you do? Why did you do that?
>
> What do you think you should have done?
>
> But if you hadn't done that, what do you think would have happened?

D Work in pairs and discuss the questions.

1 What can you learn from the mistakes you have made in the past?

2 What would you do differently if you were in the same situation in the future?

3 Is it good to talk about past mistakes?

- Talk about different versions of past events
- Talk about past mistakes

10.2 Wish lists

- Talk about your wishes and regrets
- Plan a to-do list

V reflexive verbs; staying organized **P** emphasis and reflexive pronouns **G** hopes and wishes

S bridge sentences

LISTENING

A SPEAK Work in pairs and discuss the questions.

1 Do you have any habits that you'd like to stop?
2 Are there any good habits that you'd like to start?
3 How easy is it to change your habits?
4 Look at the diagram. What do you think it shows?

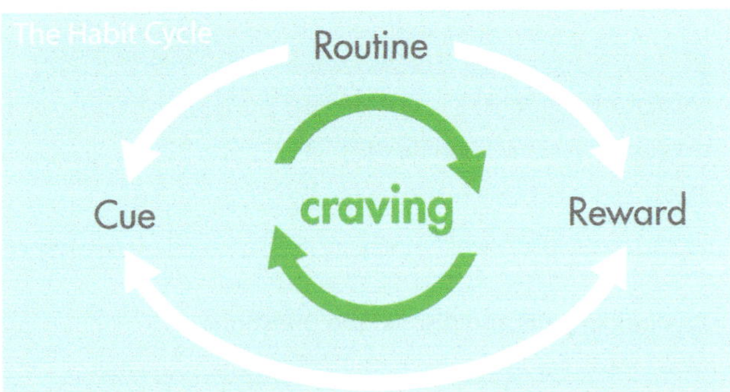

10.3 **B LISTEN FOR GIST** Listen to a radio show about habits. Which habits in the pictures do the speakers talk about?

10.3 **C LISTEN FOR DETAIL** Listen again and choose the correct answers.

1 What is David's main cue for eating fast food?
   a He sees a sign while he's driving.
   b He smells food in a shopping mall.
2 What happens when a routine is part of a true habit?
   a You can follow the steps without thinking.
   b You do it although you don't want to.
3 Why are cravings dangerous?
   a Because you don't want the reward any more.
   b Because you feel that you need the reward.
4 What's the only way to change a habit?
   a Change the routine.
   b Change the reward.
5 Why does Leo make coffee when he arrives at work?
   a Because he loves the taste of coffee.
   b Because he's tired and he needs a break.

D SPEAK Work in pairs and discuss the questions.

1 What are some cues for bad habits? What routines and rewards can we use to change those bad habits?
2 What cues and rewards can we use to start good habits?

VOCABULARY

Reflexive verbs

10.4 **A** Complete the sentences from the conversation (1–8) with the words in the box. Then listen and check your answers.

blame control get help make reward set treat

1 When I drive past a sign for a fast-food restaurant, I _______________ myself to a snack from the package.
2 'Can I try one of those?' 'Sure! _______________ yourself.'
3 I wish I could stop, but I can't _______________ myself.
4 I always _______________ myself a cup of coffee before I check my emails.
5 I suppose I could _______________ myself a glass of water.
6 I always _______________ myself goals, but nothing seems to work.
7 First of all, Alice, don't _______________ yourself.
8 How will you _______________ yourself for being good?

Reflexive verbs

A reflexive verb is a verb + a reflexive pronoun (*myself, yourself, himself, herself, itself, ourselves, yourselves, themselves*).

Some reflexive verbs have a special meaning:

Help yourself! = Please take as much as you want; there's no need to ask.

B Go to the **Vocabulary Hub** on **page XVIII**.

C **SPEAK** Work in pairs and discuss the questions.

1. Where do you see yourself in ten years?
2. How do you amuse yourself when you're on a long trip?
3. Can you think of any situations where you can't trust yourself?

PRONUNCIATION

Emphasis and reflexive pronouns

10.5 **A** Listen to the sentences from the radio show. For each sentence, decide if the reflexive pronouns are stressed or unstressed.

1. I treat myself to a snack from the package.
2. I always make myself a cup of coffee before I check my emails.
3. Don't blame yourself.
4. How will you reward yourself for being good?

B Now choose the best word or phrase to complete the rules.

Emphasis and reflexive pronouns

1. When a reflexive pronoun follows a verb, the pronoun **is / is not** usually stressed.
2. But when we want to emphasise the subject at the end of a clause, we **can / can't** stress the pronoun.

C **SPEAK** Work in pairs. Practice saying the sentences in Exercise A. Listen and check your partner's pronunciation.

GRAMMAR

Hopes and wishes

A **WORK IT OUT** Match the sentences from the conversation (1–5) with the explanations (a–d).

1. **I wish I'd known** about all this a few years ago! But I guess it's too late for me now.
2. **I hope your new routine works** for you, Leo.
3. **I wish we had time** to talk about your other seven cups of coffee, but we need to go to our next caller.
4. **I wish I could** run a marathon next year.
5. I really **wish I were** better organized.

a. The speaker is talking about something that's likely to happen in the future.
b. The speaker is talking about something that's unlikely to happen in the future.
c. The speaker is imagining a different present situation.
d. The speaker is imagining a different past situation.

Hopes and wishes

When we talk about hopes and wishes, we use very similar structures to the first, second and third conditionals.

	Conditional sentences	Hopes and wishes
Likely future	It'll be good if your idea works.	I hope your idea works.
Unlikely future	I'd be happy if I could find a new job. (or: … if I found a new job.)	I wish I could find a new job. (NOT: I wish I found a new job.)
Unreal present	It would be nice if I were taller.	I wish I were taller.
Unreal past	It would have been better if you'd told me.	I wish you'd told me.

B Go to the **Grammar Hub** on **page XIV**.

C Complete the sentences with *hope* or *wish*. Then choose the correct words to complete the hopes and wishes.

1. I ______________ you *have* / *had* / *could have* a great time on vacation next week.
2. I started playing tennis last year and I love it, but I'm too old to become a top player. I ______________ I *start* / *started* / *'d started* playing when I was younger.
3. It's great that you're coming to my city next week. I ______________ I *met* / *could meet* / *'d met* you while you're here, but unfortunately I'll be away all week.
4. I'm a little worried about Frank and Donna. They should have arrived an hour ago. I ______________ they *arrive* / *'d arrived* / *arrived* soon.
5. I never have time to do all the things I need to do each week. Sometimes I ______________ there *were* / *are* / *had been* eight days in a week!
6. My main regret is that I didn't spend enough time with my children when they were younger. I ______________ I *don't spend* / *didn't spend* / *hadn't spent* so much time working in those days!
7. My dream is to be the first person to travel to Mars! I really ______________ I *went* / *could go* / *'d gone* there one day, but I know it's never going to happen.

SPEAKING

Work in pairs and discuss the questions.

1. Do you have any regrets about your habits? What do you wish you'd started earlier? What do you wish you'd never started?
2. What do you wish you could change about yourself?
3. What are your hopes for the future? Think about next week, next month and next year.
4. What are your dreams for the future? What do you wish you could do one day?

READING

A SPEAK Work in pairs and discuss the questions.

1 What is a to-do list? What information does it contain?

2 Why do you think psychologists are interested in to-do lists?

3 Do you keep a to-do list? Why/Why not?

B READ FOR GIST Read *The psychology of to-do lists*. Match the headings (a–g) with the paragraphs (1–7).

- **a** Organization, motivation and satisfaction
- **b** The benefits of forgetting
- **c** Not as difficult as it sounds
- **d** An experiment over dinner
- **e** Keeping tasks small and simple
- **f** Using to-do lists to cut stress
- **g** The stress of not finishing things

The psychology of **to-do lists**

1 ___

One day in the 1920s, a large group of psychologists were having a meal at their favorite restaurant. They were discussing the waiter's amazing memory: he always remembered everybody's orders perfectly, but he never wrote anything down. One of the psychologists, Bluma Zeigarnik, decided to try an experiment. She told everyone to cover their plates. Then she asked the waiter to come back to the table, and to try to remember what was on each plate. Amazingly, he couldn't remember anything, even though he himself had put the plates on the table only a few minutes earlier. How was it possible that a man with such an amazing memory had forgotten everything a few minutes later?

2 ___

Zeigarnik realized that there was in fact nothing special about the waiter. In fact, we're all good at remembering current tasks – things that we still need to do. But as soon as they're finished, we forget all about them. The 'Zeigarnik effect', as it's now called, is our brains' way of cleaning up and sorting information. If we had to remember everything forever, our brains would soon run out of space.

3 ___

But there's a dark side to the Zeigarnik effect. Studies have shown that people perform badly in tests when they're worrying about other unfinished tasks. It seems that we can't stop thinking about what we still need to do. This makes us stressed and prevents us from focusing on new tasks.

4 ___

Is there anything we can do about this problem? Recent research suggests that we can reduce our stress levels by keeping a record of all our current tasks in a to-do list. This simple action tells our brains to stop worrying about the task, which means we can give our full attention to other tasks.

5 ___

To-do lists have three additional benefits. First, they help us to stay organized. Second, they are a useful record of what we've achieved and when. It can be highly motivating to look back at our past achievements – especially because the Zeigarnik effect usually makes us forget them. However, the best thing about to-do lists is the satisfying feeling you get when you cross each item off the list.

6 ___

The key to successful to-do lists is to break large objectives into smaller action points. Instead of writing 'Learn to drive' on your list, focus on small and practical jobs that you can achieve very quickly, such as 'Find a list of driving schools in my city' and 'Read a website with reviews of different schools'. The smaller the tasks, the better. Dave Allen, a time-management expert, also recommends an archive to store all the things you might need and a system of 43 folders to schedule when to do each task.

7 ___

If that sounds like too much hard work, think again. With a good system, life is much easier. You can relax and enjoy the rest of the day, happy in the knowledge that everything is under control.

Glossary

archive (n) a place where you store documents and records

C Read the box about bridge sentences. What is the connection between bridge sentences and topic sentences (see Unit 8)? What's the difference between them?

Bridge sentences

The first sentence in a paragraph is usually a bridge sentence, which shows how the paragraph is connected to the previous paragraph. For example, it might use words like *however* to introduce a contrast, or words like *another* to add extra information.

Not all paragraphs have a bridge sentence.

D READ FOR KEY INFORMATION Read the first sentence in each paragraph again. Which five are bridge sentences? Underline the words and phrases in the sentences that refer back to the previous paragraph. What exactly do they refer to?

E SPEAK Work in pairs and discuss the questions.

1 Have you ever experienced the Zeigarnik effect? Think about:
- preparing for a test.
- learning a speech, a song or a poem.
- remembering people's names and faces.

2 Do you ever look back at your past achievements? Would you find it motivating?

VOCABULARY

Staying organized

A Look at the underlined words in *The psychology of to-do lists*. Find words or phrases that mean the following.

1 a job that you need to do
a t a s k

2 to keep something in a safe place
to _ _ _ _ _ something

3 to put things back in the right places
to _ _ _ _ _ up

4 to plan exactly when you will do something
to _ _ _ _ _ _ _ _ something

5 a small thing that you're going to do
an _ _ _ _ _ _ point

6 to put things in the right order
to _ _ _ _ things

7 a large thing that you want to achieve
an _ _ _ _ _ _ _ _ _

8 to write something down
to keep a _ _ _ _ _ _ of something

B SPEAK Work in pairs and discuss the questions.

1 How many **tasks** are on your to-do list?

2 Do you **keep a record** of the tasks you need to do? Would you like to start?

SPEAKING HUB

A PREPARE Write a short wish list. Use the ideas below or your own ideas.
- a problem that you would like to solve
- a good habit that you hope you will start / wish you could start
- a way to become less stressed or better organized
- how you'll continue learning/using English after this course

B PLAN Work in groups. Discuss your wish lists. As a group, choose the most interesting items from your wish lists and create a to-do list. Try to:
- plan cues, routines and rewards for any habits you want to change.
- turn your objectives into tasks and action points.

C PRESENT Stand up and tell the class what you plan to do and when. When others are speaking, listen carefully and be positive about their plans.

D REFLECT Work in groups and discuss the questions.

1 How will you make sure you'll do the things on your list?

2 How will you motivate each other to do those things?

Talk about your wishes and regrets
Plan a to-do list

10.3 Come home

F make and accept apologies   P vowel sounds

COMPREHENSION

A When was the last time you had to say goodbye to someone? How did you feel? How long was it before you saw that person again?

B Number the pictures in the order you think they happened. What do you think happened?

a ☐

b ☐

c ☐

d ☐

e ☐

f ☐

C ▶ 00:00–02:25 Watch the first part of the video and check your ideas. How do you think the video will end?

D ▶ 02:25–04:29 Complete the letter that Sam wrote to Gaby by choosing the correct words below. Watch the second part of the video and check your answers. Does the video end how you predicted?

1 leaving / in / over
2 words / time / pen
3 should / usually / never
4 city / life / home
5 business / Madrid / yourself

Dear Gaby,

I've just heard that you're [1] ______________ London and … I wish I had said this to you in person, but I just couldn't find the [2] ______________. I'm so sorry, but I [3] ______________ know the right thing to say. I know you've already made your mind up about leaving, and I'm going to miss you so much. The thought of not having you in my [4] ______________ hurts because … I love you. I always have. I just didn't know how to say it before. Take good care of [5] ______________.

MILLY

SAM

NEENA

ZAC

GABY

FUNCTIONAL LANGUAGE

Making and accepting apologies

A Put the words in the correct order. Then put each phrase under the correct heading in the table.

1 quickly / leave / sorry / to / so / I'm / really

____

2 you'll / worry / be / don't / fine

____

3 apologize / need / no / there's / to

____

4 worry / don't / it / about

____

5 just / things / of / those / one / it's

____

6 OK / all / to / be / it's / going

____

7 my / it's / fault

____

8 not / fault / fault / it's / it's / my / your

____

9 nothing / about / worry / there's / to

____

10 great / is / this / to / be / going

____

Making an apology	Accepting an apology	Giving reassurance
I'm really sorry to leave so quickly.		

B Watch the video again and check (✓) each phrase as you hear it.

Glossary

housemate **(n) (British)** = roommate **(n) (American)**

USEFUL PHRASES

A Match the useful phrases (1–5) with the phrases that come before or after them (a–e).

1 It's time to go.
2 I wish I had said this to you in person.
3 I'm such an idiot!
4 I've changed my mind about leaving.
5 I'm scared.

a What about your plane? You're going to miss it.
b I can't believe that I missed her.
c You'll be fine; don't worry.
d But I just couldn't find the words.
e There's nothing to worry about.

B How do you say these useful phrases in your language?

PRONUNCIATION

Vowel sounds

A Match words with the same vowel sounds from boxes A, B and C.

A airport roommate <u>mind</u> person sorry worry

B apologize <u>guys</u> hurt love strangely thought

C gone <u>my</u> of course paying under words

10.6 **B** Listen, check and repeat the words. Copy the sounds.

SPEAKING

A Work in pairs. Write conversations about the following situations or your own ideas. Student A – apologize. Student B – accept the apology and reassure Student A.

arrive late / for meeting break / chair
forget / to call miss / party spill / coffee

A: I'm really sorry about breaking your chair.
B: Oh, don't worry about it – it's not your fault. It's just one of those things.

B PRESENT Act out your conversations. Take turns being Student A and Student B.

Make and accept apologies

➤ Turn to page XXVIII to learn how to write a report.

Unit 10 Review

GRAMMAR

A Complete the third conditional sentences. Use the correct form of the underlined verbs.

1 The waiter forgot our order because he didn't write it down.
If the waiter ___had written___ down our order, he ___wouldn't have forgotten___ it.

2 You didn't finish anything on your to-do list. Maybe it's because all the items were too big.
You might ______ some things on your to-do list if they ______ a little smaller.

3 I saw a sign for a fast-food restaurant, so I felt a need to eat.
If I ______ a sign for the fast-food restaurant, I ______ a need to eat!

4 I didn't have time to try on these jeans, but I bought them anyway.
I ______ these jeans if I ______ them on first! They're much too small!

B Write sentences with *should/shouldn't have done*.

1 I wish you'd been more careful.
You ___should have been more careful___.

2 I regret buying these shoes.
I ______.

3 Why didn't they listen to us?
They ______.

4 It was a mistake to go out yesterday.
We ______.

C Complete the conversation with the correct form of the verbs in parentheses.

A: Hey! I'm having a dinner party tomorrow night. I hope you [1] ______ (*can come*). It's going to be excellent.

B: Oh, I wish I [2] ______ (*can come*), but I can't. I have tickets for a soccer game tomorrow, and it's the final.

A: Oh, I didn't know it's the final tomorrow! I wish I [3] ______ (*know*)! I'd have arranged the party for a different night. Anyway, I hope your team [4] ______ (*win*)!

B: Well, my team isn't in the final. I wish we [5] ______ (*be*)! But we lost in the semi-final last week. I wish I [6] ______ (*not buy*) a ticket – then I could come to your party!

VOCABULARY

A Choose the correct verbs to complete the sentences.

1 I got an email from somebody who tried to ***persuade / trick*** me into giving my bank account number.

2 I didn't want to buy a camera at all, but the saleswoman ***affected / persuaded*** me to buy one.

3 Whenever I walk past a fast-food restaurant, I'm ***regretted / tempted*** to go inside.

4 For a long time, businesses ***assumed / influenced*** that more choice meant more sales.

B Find and correct one mistake in each underlined phrase.

[1]Would you mind that I asked you for some advice? You see, I want to go somewhere new this weekend, but I'm [2]of three minds about where to go. This morning, I [3]made my mind and decided to go bike riding in the forest, but then I heard the weather is going to be horrible, so I [4]changed the mind and decided to go to the new museum instead. But … I don't really like museums. What should I do? [5]Bear to mind, I don't have a car, so it needs to be somewhere with good bus connections.

C Match the beginnings of the tips for staying organized (1–5) with the endings (a–e).

1 Don't do everything at once. Focus
2 Remember to schedule
3 Use a to-do list to keep
4 Break big objectives into smaller action
5 Use an archive to store

a a record of your tasks.
b important old documents.
c some time to relax!
d on one task at a time.
e points.

D Choose the correct reflexive verb to complete the sentences.

1 You shouldn't ***blame / control*** yourself. It's not your fault.

2 ***Help / get*** yourself to anything you want.

3 I always go into fast food restaurants when I see them. I can't ***make / control*** myself.

4 He's trained so hard for the race. Why doesn't he ***treat / set*** himself to a night off and just relax?

FUNCTIONAL LANGUAGE

Complete the conversation with the words in the box. There are two extra words.

about	apologize	blame	fault	not	so	those	worry

Dimitri: Hey, Igor! Have you eaten my pizza?

Igor: Don't [1] ______ me! I've been out all day. I don't know anything about it.

Dimitri: Oh … I'm [2] ______ sorry. I shouldn't have blamed you.

Igor: It's OK. Don't [3] ______ about it. So I wonder who ate your pizza …

Rob: Uh, sorry, but it's my [4] ______. I was really hungry when I got home last night and I hadn't gone to the store!

Dimitri: Oh, there's no need to [5] ______. It's just one of [6] ______ things.

Endmatter Contents

Grammar Hub

Unit 6	VI–VII
Unit 7	VIII–IX
Unit 8	X–XI
Unit 9	XII–XIII
Unit 10	XIV–XV

Vocabulary Hub

6.2 Hobbies and free time activities	XVI
7.1 Phrasal verbs	XVI
7.1 Adjectives to describe food	XVII
8.2 Positive adjectives	XVII
9.1 Verbal idioms	XVIII
10.2 Reflexive verbs	XVIII

Communication Hub

6.2 Student A	XIX
6.2 Student B	XXIII
7.2 Students A and B	XX
8.3 Student A	XX
8.3 Student B	XXII
9.1 Student B	XXI
9.1 Student C	XXII
9.2 Student A	XIX
9.2 Student B	XXI
10.1 Students A and B	XXIII

Writing

Unit 6	XXIV
Unit 7	XXV
Unit 8	XXVI
Unit 9	XXVII
Unit 10	XXVIII

Audio scripts	XXIX–XXXIV

Grammar Hub

6.1 Modals of obligation

should

	Positive	Negative
I/you/he/she/it/we/they	**I should choose** the best team.	**We shouldn't yell** at the players.

must

	Positive	Negative
I/you/he/she/it/we/they	**They must find** a better place to train.	**You must not be** so aggressive on the field.

have to

	Positive	Negative
I/you/we/they	**You have to wear** a helmet.	**They don't have to play** the game on the computer.
he/she/it	**She has to perform** well today.	**He doesn't have to win** every match.

- We use *should/shouldn't* when we describe what is or is not a good idea now, in the future or generally.
- We use *must* and *have to* when we describe rules and situations that are necessary.
- There is sometimes no difference between them. However, we usually use *must* and *must not* in written rules, and *have to* in speech.
- We use *must not* when we describe something that is not allowed.
- We use *don't/doesn't have to* when we describe things that aren't necessary, but you may still do them.
- There is a difference in meaning between *must not* and *don't have to*.

  must not *= not allowed*

  don't have to *= not necessary*
- In questions, we use *have to* instead of *must*.
- We can use *don't/doesn't need to* instead of *don't/doesn't have to* when we describe things that aren't necessary.

6.2 Present perfect and present perfect progressive; *had to / needed to*

Present perfect

Positive	Negative	Question
I've joined a sailing club.	**They haven't made up** their minds about joining the league.	**Have you met** your opponent yet?

- We use the present perfect for actions completed during a period of time that continues to now.
- We also use the present perfect for actions completed before now when we don't say exactly when.
- See Grammar Hub 2.1 for more information about the present perfect.

Present perfect progressive

	Positive	Negative
I/you/we/they	**I have been collecting** stamps for years.	**We haven't been doing** our best in every game.
he/she/it	**She's been training** hard every single day.	**Zain hasn't been training** hard enough.

Question	Positive short answer	Negative short answer
Have they been playing tennis for long?	Yes, **they have**.	No, **they haven't**.
Has Anika been watching the game on TV?	Yes, **she has**.	No, **she hasn't**.

- We use the present perfect progressive to talk about an action that started in the past and continues in the present. It can be a single or a frequently repeated action.

  He has been cooking all afternoon.
- We can use both the present perfect and the present perfect progressive to describe a recently completed activity.

  She has posted the videos on social media. She has been posting the videos on social media all morning.
- We use the present perfect progressive to find out the duration of an activity.

  How long have you been waiting for your teammates?
- We do NOT use the present perfect progressive with state verbs.

  I have known my coach for years.

had to / needed to

	Positive	Negative
I/you/he/she/it/we/they	**They had to** practice for four hours each day.	**You didn't have to train** for the snowball fight.
	He needed to wear safety equipment.	**She didn't need to buy** a new helmet.

Question	Positive short answer	Negative short answer
Did you have to take a lesson first?	Yes, **I/we did**.	No, **I/we didn't**.

- We use *had to* and *needed to* to talk about things that were necessary in the past. They mean the same thing.
- We don't use *must* to talk about the past.

  They had to pay for the skiing lessons last winter.
- We use *didn't have to* and *didn't need to* to talk about things that were not necessary but possible in the past.

6.1 Modals of obligation

A Choose the correct option.

1 We *don't have to* / *must not* be competitive to have fun playing sports.
2 He *must* / *doesn't have to* wear a helmet. It's required.
3 I *must* / *must not* eat a massive meal before playing a sport.
4 They *shouldn't* / *don't have to* practice today because the coach isn't going to be here.
5 *Do you have to* / *Must you* train every day?

B Complete the sentences with the correct words and phrases from the box.

don't have doesn't have has must not don't need should

1 You ________________ to buy a ticket. Dad's bought them already.
2 She ________________ ask her coach for advice on how to play better.
3 I ________________ to go to practice today. It's been canceled.
4 For a helmet to work, it ________________ to fit on your head properly.
5 You ________________ run while holding the ball. It's against the rules.
6 He ________________ to wear protective gear because his sport isn't dangerous.

C Choose the correct option to complete the dialogue.

Anna: I'm excited about Saturday's game. It starts at 1 pm. I think we [1] ________________ meet in front of the entrance, shouldn't we?

Vincenzo: I [2] ________________ take my little sister to her lesson first, so I might be a little late. You [3] ________________ wait for me outside. Just go on inside and I'll find you.

Anna: Well, I don't mind waiting for you outside. I [4] ________________ be in my seat when the game starts. Besides, it's a big place. We [5] ________________ go in together so we don't get lost.

Vincenzo: OK, fine.

	a	b	c
1	don't need to	must	should
2	have to	should	don't have to
3	must	don't have to	have to
4	should	must	don't have to
5	must	should	don't need to

➤ Go back to page 63.

6.2 Present perfect and present perfect progressive; *had to / needed to*

A Choose the correct option.

1 I've never *played* / *been playing* racquetball before. Is it fun?
2 Have you *been watching* / *watched* sports on TV all day?
3 I've just *finished* / *been finishing* a really difficult exercise class.
4 Sorry about my appearance. I've *run* / *been running*.
5 Do you think he's *understood* / *been understanding* the rules yet?
6 Lee hasn't *worked out* / *been working out* for a long time but he's already *increased* / *been increasing* his muscle strength.

B Complete the sentences in the present perfect or progressive with the correct form of these verbs. Sometimes more than one tense is possible.

follow join stay lose play spend

1 Tom has ____lost____ interest in playing soccer.
2 The coach has ________________ a lot of time with the players lately.
3 Have you ________________ the tennis competition? It's getting good!
4 Georgia has ________________ in shape these days using a new exercise program.
5 Eli and Greta haven't ________________ the club yet.
6 I've ________________ this video game all day and there's still a lot left.

C Correct the mistakes.

1 He had to ~~left~~ leave the game because he broke his leg.
2 I must yell so the other players could hear me.
3 You hadn't to yell. I couldn't hear you on the field.
4 I didn't needed to tell my friend about the game.
5 **A:** Why they didn't have to buy a paddle?
B: Because they already had one.

➤ Go back to page 69.

Grammar Hub

7.1 Modals of speculation and deduction

- We use *could*, *might* or *may* when we think something is possible, but we are not sure.

  This dish is very hot – it could contain a lot of chilies.
  Carla might be allergic to nuts – don't add any walnuts.
  Paul may want sugar in his coffee.

- In the negative, we use *might not* and *may not* but NOT *could not*.

  This restaurant may/might not be very good.
  NOT ~~This restaurant could not be very good.~~

- We use *must* when we are sure something is true because we have strong evidence for our belief.

  This cake is burned – it must taste horrible!

- We use *can't* when we are sure something is not true because we have strong evidence for our belief.

  These cookies are white – they can't be chocolate chip cookies.

- We don't use *must* and *can't* for facts we are 100% sure about.

7.2 Comparatives and superlatives; *the …, the …*

Comparatives and superlatives

	Comparative	Superlative
Short adjectives (one syllable)	adj + *-er* (+ *than*) cheap → cheap**er**	*the* + adj + *-est* cheap → **the** cheap**est**
Longer adjectives	*more* + adj (+ *than*) popular → **more** popular	*the most* + adj popular → **the most** popular
Irregular adjectives	good → **better** (+ *than*) bad → **worse** (+ *than*)	good → **the best** bad → **the worst**
Adverbs	*more* + adv (+ *than*) quickly → **more** quickly	*the most* + adv quickly → **the most** quickly
Irregular adverbs	badly → **worse** far → **farther/further** fast → fast**er** hard → hard**er** well → **better**	badly → **the worst** far → **the farthest** / **the furthest** fast → **the** fast**est** hard → **the** hard**est** well → **the best**
Countable nouns	many nutrients → **more** nutrients few nutrients → few**er** nutrients	many nutrients → **the most** nutrients few nutrients → **the** few**est** nutrients
Uncountable nouns	much protein → **more** protein little fiber → **less** fiber	much protein → **the most** protein little fiber → **the least** fiber

- We use comparative adjectives and adverbs to say how two or more things or actions are different.
- We use superlative adjectives and adverbs to say that something is the top or bottom of a group.
- For adjectives ending in *-e* or *-y* the rules differ a little.

  Your meal is larger than mine, but Harry's is the largest.
  Carrot soup is tastier than pea soup, but chicken soup is the tastiest of all.

- For adjectives which end with one vowel and one consonant, we double the final consonant before adding *-er* or *-est*.

  *These melons are **bigger** than those ones.*

- To make negative comparatives and superlatives, we use *less* instead of *more* and *the least* instead of *the most*.
- We never use *more* or *the most* together with *-er* or *-est*.

  I think juice is healthier than coffee. NOT ~~I think juice is more healthier than coffee.~~

- We only use *than* when it is followed by the thing we are comparing.

  This dish is good but this one is better. NOT ~~This dish is good but this one is better than.~~
  This dish is better than that dish.

the …, the …

the + comparative adjective + noun, *the* + comparative adjective + noun	**The fresher** the ingredients, **the better** the dish.
the + comparative adjective + clause, *the* + comparative adjective + clause	**The more tasty** it is, **the more satisfied** they will be.
the + comparative adverb + clause, *the* + comparative adverb + clause	**The faster** it boils, **the more quickly** it will be ready.
the + *more/less* + noun + clause, *the* + *more/less* + noun + clause	**The more recipes** you learn, **the more food** you can cook.
the + *more/less* + clause, *the* + *more/less* + clause	**The more I practiced**, **the less I needed** a cookbook.

- We use *the …, the* to show that two changes are closely connected. As one thing changes, the other thing changes too.
- Sometimes we use the very simplest form of this structure, using comparative adjectives only, and no verb.

  The more, the merrier.

- We don't have to use only the forms shown in the table above. We can also combine different parts of the structures.

  The more complicated the recipe, the longer it takes.
  The less we spend on food, the more money we have.

7.1 Modals of speculation and deduction

A Decide if the statements are true or false.

1 'Kitty may serve fruit salad for dessert tonight.'
Dessert will definitely be fruit salad. **True / False**

2 'I've been invited to three pot-luck dinners. They must be popular.'
Pot-luck dinners are popular. **True / False**

3 'This can't be tomato soup – it isn't red!'
It almost certainly isn't tomato soup. **True / False**

4 'Bitter chocolate could be good in a cake.'
The speaker really doesn't like bitter chocolate. **True / False**

5 'If you left the milk out all night, it could be sour.'
It's possible that the milk is sour. **True / False**

B Choose the correct option.

1 **A:** 'Are you going to order soup?'
B: 'No, I'm very hungry and it ***must not / might not*** be very filling.'

2 **A:** 'Lara said she wants chicken.'
B: 'But she doesn't eat meat. She ***can't / must not*** want chicken.'

3 **A:** 'What's 'scampi'?'
B: 'I don't know really. It ***could / can*** be some kind of fish.'

4 **A:** 'Dinner is at seven tonight.'
B: 'I ***could / may*** not get there in time because I have to work late.'

5 **A:** 'Look at that man! He's ordered three pizzas!'
B: 'He ***can / must*** really like pizza!'

6 **A:** 'I've ordered sushi for lunch.'
B: 'Hector ***might / could*** not eat that but we'll see.'

➤ Go back to page 77.

7.2 Comparatives and superlatives; *the …, the …*

A Complete the sentences with the correct form of the adjectives and adverbs in parentheses.

1 The ________________ (*fast*) the pizza delivery man can get here is 15 minutes.

2 You can buy cheese ________________ (*cheaply*) in the street market than in the stores.

3 The food in the airport was bad, but the meal on the plane was ________________ (*bad*).

4 I made the soup with ________________ (*few*) ingredients than it says in the recipe.

5 The ________________ (*good*) way to serve this dessert is with a little cream.

6 I would prefer to try a ________________ (*mild*) sauce than the one you're eating.

B Complete the sentences with the words and phrases in the box.

less meat	more times	more quickly	the better	the more money	the sweeter	you disagree

1 The ________________ you eat, the healthier it is for your heart.

2 The more sugar you add, ________________ the sauce will be.

3 The ________________ you eat your salad, the sooner you'll have dessert!

4 The more ________________ with me, the less likely I am to change my mind!

5 The ________________ you reheat food, the more unsafe it becomes.

6 The less food we throw away, ________________ we'll save.

➤ Go back to page 80.

C Correct the mistakes in each sentence.

1 The peas will cook more fast than the potatoes.

2 I think the most sourest taste of any food is vinegar.

3 Salad is the least filling than pasta.

4 First prize in the competition will go to the person who cooks the more creatively.

5 I put very little sugar in Jim's coffee, but he wanted even little!

6 Chia seeds have much protein than some foods, but quinoa has the most.

D Write one word in each blank to complete the sentences.

1 Is fast food ________________ popular than home cooking in your country?

2 My old mixer worked fairly well, but this one works much ________________.

3 Water is the ________________ fattening drink you can have because it has zero calories!

4 Raw food is generally healthier ________________ cooked food.

5 All these curries are spicy, but this one is the hottest ________________ all!

6 The older the wine is, ________________ better it gets.

7 The salad plates are pretty large, but the dinner plates are ________________.

8 Mmm! This is ________________ most delicious meal I've ever had!

➤ Go back to page 81.

Grammar Hub

8.1 Adjective clauses

Essential adjective clauses

	Relative pronoun	
Person	who/that	The person **who/that** first had the idea was named Smith.
Thing	which/that	The thing **which/that** stops it being a success is the price.
Possession	whose	The man **whose** design won first prize was from China.
Place	where	The company **where** I work makes a difference to people's lives.
Time	when	Early in the morning is the time **when** I have my best ideas.

- We use an essential adjective clause to give information about and identify a noun (person or thing).
- We use *who* or *that* for people, and *which* or *that* for things.
- With *who*, *which* and *that*, we can leave out the relative pronoun if it's followed by a subject + verb rather than just a verb.

  The design (that) he suggested was very good.
- When the relative pronoun is the subject of the adjective clause, we don't add another pronoun.

  *Do you know the name of the man **who invented** this?* NOT *~~Do you know the name of the man who he invented this?~~*

Non-essential adjective clauses

	Relative pronoun	
Person	who	Carol Taylor, **who** presents science programs, is a university professor.
Thing	which	The idea, **which** I first read about in the newspaper, is really very simple.
Possession	whose	Miriam, **whose** dad is a designer, would like to become an inventor.
Place	where	London, **where** her grandparents live, is where Sophie would like to find work.
Time	when	On Sundays, **when** Andrew isn't working, he likes to catch up with his reading.

- We use a non-essential adjective clause when we want to include two pieces of information in the same sentence. The adjective clause is usually an additional piece of information and is always separated by commas.
- We do not use *that* with non-essential adjective clauses.
- When we remove a non-essential adjective clause, the sentence still makes sense.

8.2 Zero and first conditionals; Conditionals with modals and imperatives

Zero conditional

Condition	Result
If **you listen**,	**you learn**.
If **you like** science,	**it helps**.

Question	Positive short answer	Negative short answer
If **I win**, **do I get** a prize?	Yes, **you do**.	No, **you don't**.
Does it help if you like science?	Yes, **it does**.	No, **it doesn't**.

- We use the zero conditional to talk about things that are always true.
- We can put the *if*-clause or the result clause first. The only difference is we do not use a comma if we begin with the result clause.
- We can use negatives and *unless* (which means *if not* or *except if*) in the zero conditional.

  If you don't pay attention, you make mistakes.
  = Unless you pay attention, you make mistakes.

First conditional

Condition	Result
If **you try** hard,	**you'll succeed**.
If **it doesn't work**,	**we'll start** again.

Question	Positive short answer	Negative short answer
If **we win** the award, **will we be** famous?	Yes, **we/you will**.	No, **we/you won't**.
Will we be famous if **we win** the award?		

- We use the first conditional to talk about possible situations in the future.
- We can put the *if*-clause or the result clause first. The only difference is we do not use a comma if we begin with the result clause.
- We can use negatives and *unless* (meaning *if not* or *except if*) in the first conditional.

  If you don't listen, you won't understand.
  = Unless you listen, you won't understand.
- We never put *will* in an *if*-clause.

Conditionals with modals and imperatives

- We can use other modal verbs (e.g. *can*, *could*, *might*, *should*) instead of *will*.

  *If you work hard enough, you **can** do it!*
  *I **might** visit the science museum if it's open tomorrow.*
- We can use an imperative instead of a result clause.

  *If you see smoke, **call** for help.*
  ***Call** me if you have any questions.*

8.1 Adjective clauses

A Choose the correct option.

1 There are a lot of students ***which*** / ***who*** have great ideas.
2 The last century was the time ***when*** / ***where*** technology really progressed.
3 The magazine ***who*** / ***that*** I like best is called *New Scientist*.
4 Princeton is the place ***where*** / ***which*** I studied for my degree.
5 I want to find a job ***that*** / ***who*** helps others.
6 John is the boy ***who*** / ***whose*** father is a doctor.
7 I don't know anyone ***who*** / ***which*** works in technology.
8 He was born at a time ***when*** / ***where*** computers didn't exist.

B Match to make sentences.

1 California is where b
2 The computer is an invention ___
3 Steve Jobs was the person who ___
4 The experiences ___
5 Myra is the woman ___
6 My phone is the one thing ___
7 I really enjoyed the time ___

a started Apple Computers.
b most software industries started.
c which I would hate to lose.
d which has changed many people's lives.
e that I had were more important than the money I made.
f when I was studying at college.
g who helped me choose my career.

C **Join the two sentences to make one. Use non-essential adjective clauses.**

1 My aunt is a scientist. She lives in Boston.
My aunt, who lives in Boston, is a scientist. / My aunt, who is a scientist, lives in Boston.
2 The invention is very simple. It has made a big difference to people's lives.
___
3 Justin is 23. He has just won a prize.
___
4 Carl spoke to us from Lisbon. He lives there.
___
5 The invention won first prize. It is sold in many countries.
___
6 Marie loves inventing things. Her husband is also an engineer.
___
7 Next week the results come out. We'll see if you win anything.
___

➤ Go back to page 87.

8.2 Zero and first conditionals; Conditionals with modals and imperatives

A **Find and correct the mistakes with the zero conditional.**

1 If you ~~will~~ read a lot, you understand things better.
2 It's better if you called me in the evenings.
3 Unless you don't try, you don't learn.
4 The roads will more dangerous if it rains.
5 It doesn't work if you won't turn it on.
6 I'll never go out if it's cold.

B **Complete the first conditional sentences using the information in parentheses.**

1 The machine will not work *if you don't press this button.*
(*you / not / press this button*)
2 If you find it at the right price, ___
(*you / buy it?*)
3 What will we do ___
(*it / not work?*)
4 How will you get home ___
(*you / miss the bus?*)
5 If it rains tomorrow, ___
(*you / still / play soccer?*)
6 If you take an umbrella with you, ___
(*it / keep you dry*)
7 I won't help him ___
(*he / not ask*)

➤ Go back to page 91.

C **Choose the correct option.**

1 If you see Jimmy, ___
a will give him this note.
(b) give him this note.
2 You will save money if ___
a you can wait a few months.
b you will wait a few months.
3 If you don't like it, ___
a you can go home.
b will you go home.
4 If you have any problems, ___
a will call me.
b call me.
5 If I feel like it, ___
a I might go to the pop concert.
b I can go to the pop concert.
6 Ask me if there's anything ___
a you don't understand.
b you won't understand.
7 If you want to have a good time, ___
a you will come and join us on Saturday night!
b come and join us on Saturday night!

➤ Go back to page 93.

Grammar Hub

9.1 Second conditional

Condition	Result
If **you submitted** a proposal,	**they would accept** it.
If **she didn't teach** music,	**she'd be** a full-time musician.
If **the show were** expensive,	**I wouldn't go** to it.
If **we didn't have** an art venue,	**we wouldn't see** much art.

Question	Positive short answer	Negative short answer
If **you had** more free time, **would you spend** it creatively?	Yes, **I would**.	No, **I wouldn't**.
Would you spend your free time creatively if **you had** more of it?		

- We use the second conditional to talk about present situations that aren't real and future events that are unlikely but possible.
- Although it uses the simple past, the second conditional is NOT about the past.
- We use *if* + simple past in the *if*-clause and *would* + base form in the result clause.
- We can use *might* or *could* in the result clause if we are not sure of the result.

  If she rehearsed every day, she might improve her skills.

  We could display community art if we had a local arts venue.
- With the verb *be*, we generally use *were* instead of *was* with all subjects, including *I*.

9.2 Reported speech

Direct speech	Reported speech
simple present	simple past
'**We enjoy** live concerts the best.'	They said (that) **they enjoyed** live concerts the best.
present progressive	past progressive
'**We are learning** how to write a short story.'	They said (that) **they were learning** how to write a short story.
will	*would*
'**I will** read my book later.'	She said (that) **she would** read her book later.
may	*might*
'**Elle may** sing in the play.'	He said (that) **Elle might** sing in the play.
can	*could*
'**We can** film our daily lives.'	They said (that) **they could** film their daily lives.
should	*should* (no change)
'**He should try out** for that role.'	She said (that) he **should try out** for that role.
For commands and instructions	*tell* + object (+ *not*) + infinitive
'**Rehearse** the scene again.'	He told them **to rehearse** the scene again.
'**Don't look** at the camera.'	She told me **not to look** at the camera.

- We use reported speech to report what people say. We use a reporting verb in the simple past (e.g. *said*, *asked*, *told*).
- When we report what someone says, the reported verb usually goes back one tense.
- When we report questions, the subject comes before the verb (the same as in sentences).

  *Alain: 'Where **is he acting**?' → Alain asked where **he was acting**.*
- With yes/no questions, we start the reported question with *if* or *whether*.

  *Chloe: 'Will Tom attend the show?' → Chloe asked **if/whether** Tom would attend the show.*
- We change some pronouns from direct speech to reported speech depending on the speaker (*I* to *he/she*, *you* to *me*, *my* to *his/her*, etc).

  *Kieran: 'I've given **you my** ticket already.' → He said **he** had given **me his** ticket already.*
- We sometimes also need to change words which refer to time and place.

Direct speech	Reported speech
tomorrow	*the next day / the following day*
today	*that day*
here	*there*
this	*that/the*

- We usually don't change the verb tenses if we are reporting facts that are still true in the present.

  *Our coach said that acting **requires** a great deal of time and effort.*

9.1 Second conditional

A Choose the correct option.

1 If I *knew* / *know* the words to the song, I would sing it.
2 If she had a better idea for the story, she *uses* / *would use* it.
3 If we *would hold* / *held* an art competition, many people would take part.
4 The public *liked* / *might like* his proposal if he presented it to them.
5 If you *invite* / *invited* Monique to the play, would she come?
6 If they allowed the public behind the stage, the actors *weren't* / *wouldn't be* pleased.
7 I'd study art at Kingston University if I *were* / *am* you.

B Correct the mistakes in these second conditional sentences.

1 If you ~~get~~ got rid of your guitar, you would miss it later.
2 If we bought cheaper tickets, we would saved a lot of money.
3 If they interact with the audience, the play would be more exciting.
4 I won't be terribly upset if my bandmates and I didn't make up.
5 Will Chanda enjoy it more if she spent more time in her studio?
6 If the show took place outdoors, more people can come.
7 Everyone would be very unhappy if it rains the day of the concert.

C Write the correct form of the verbs in parentheses. Use *would* if necessary.

1 If the city ___built___ (*build*) a new theater, many people would attend it.
2 If we rehearsed every day, we ______________ (*become*) the best!
3 If my favorite musician ______________ (*perform*) for free, thousands would go to see it.
4 Jean-Philippe ______________ (*sell*) millions of copies if he recorded his songs.
5 The public would be disappointed if the gallery ______________ (*close*) its doors.
6 If I ______________ (*be*) a famous artist, could I sell my paintings for $1 million?
7 If you ______________ (*tell*) your story, I think people would show an interest in it.
8 Most people ______________ (*not like*) it if I sang in public!

➤ Go back to page 99.

9.2 Reported speech

A Choose the correct option.

1 Maya: 'I'm going to an outdoor concert tonight.'
She said she *is* / *was* going to an outdoor concert that night.
2 Dan and Tracy: 'We're rehearsing all day tomorrow.'
They said they *were rehearsing* / *will rehearse* all day the following day.
3 Joe to Lyn: 'I can give you my proposal.'
He said he *can* / *could* give her his proposal.
4 Nadia to me: 'I will ask the doorman to let you in for free.'
She said she *asked* / *would ask* the doorman to let me in for free.
5 The teachers: 'We've chosen a local warehouse.'
They said they *will choose* / *had chosen* a local warehouse.
6 Me: 'I'm not writing a review of the play this evening.'
You said you weren't writing the review *this* / *that* evening.
7 John to Isabel: 'Come to the concert hall at 7 pm.'
John *said* / *told* Isabel to come to the concert hall at 7 pm.

B Report the statements.

1 Hanna: 'I'm performing at the theater tomorrow.'
She said _(that) she was performing at the theater the next/following day._
2 Alexis: 'I've never written a novel before.'
He said ______________
3 Marcia: 'I'll buy my tickets online.'
She said ______________
4 Davide and Maria: 'We're meeting a famous actor today.'
They said ______________
5 Anastasiya: 'I can't hear from the back row.'
She said ______________
6 Hussein: 'I gave Sonia my seat.'
He said ______________

C Choose the correct option.

1 Sara: 'When is the concert?'
She asked ______________.
a if the concert was today
b when the concert was
c when is the concert

2 Elena to Jim: 'You'll love Paulina's performance.'
She promised that Jim ______________ Paulina's performance.
a loves
b will love
c would love

3 Soraya to me: 'Have you read *The Great Gatsby*?'
She asked me ______________ *The Great Gatsby*.
a whether I read
b if I had read
c why I had read

4 Georgia and Hans: 'Are our seats at the front?'
They asked ______________.
a if our seats are at the front
b if our seats were at the front
c if their seats were at the front

➤ Go back to page 103.

Grammar Hub

10.1 Third conditional; *would have* + past participle

Third conditional

Condition	Result
I would have made a better decision	if **Daniel had done** the research.
If **I had known** all the facts,	**he wouldn't have made** his discovery.

Question	Positive short answer	Negative short answer
If **you had thought** about it more, **would you have made** the same decision?	Yes, **I would (have)**.	No, **I wouldn't (have)**.
Would they have passed the exam if **they had answered** correctly?	Yes, **they would (have)**.	No, **they wouldn't (have)**.

- We use the third conditional to imagine a situation in the past that didn't actually happen.

  *If I had set my alarm clock, I wouldn't have been late for work. (= I **didn't** set my alarm clock and I **was** late for work.)*
- As with other conditionals, we only use a comma when the *if*-clause comes first.
- We can use *could have* or *might have* instead of *would have* to express possibility.

  I could have answered correctly if I'd had more time.
- In answer to a third conditional question, we can use either *I would* or *I would have*.

  Would you have made the same decision if you'd known all the facts?
  Yes, I would. / Yes, I would have. / No, I wouldn't. / No, I wouldn't have.

would have + past participle

should have + past participle

Positive	Negative	Question
I would have told her about my exam results.	**He wouldn't have bought** me such an expensive gift.	**Why would they have left** the house already?
She should have bought the first pair.	**You shouldn't have spent** so much money.	**Should I have changed** my mind?
They should have offered more choice.	**I shouldn't have bought** these shoes.	How much **should they have paid**?

- We use *should/shouldn't have* + the past participle of the main verb to talk about mistakes that we made in the past. We regret those actions and try to imagine how we could have acted differently.

  *She shouldn't have changed her mind. (= She **did** change her mind and this was a mistake.)*
- We always put the past participle of the main verb after *should/shouldn't have*.

  They should have thought about their decision more carefully. NOT ~~They should have think about their decision more carefully.~~

10.2 Hopes and wishes

wish + simple past	imagining a different present situation (unreal present)	**I wish she were** more organized. **I wish I weren't** so hungry! **He wishes he knew** the answer.
wish + past perfect	imagining a different past situation (unreal past)	**We wish our son had won** the race. **They wish they hadn't eaten** so much.
wish + *could*	imagining an unlikely future possibility (unlikely future)	**I wish I could stop** drinking coffee.
hope (that) + simple present/ present progressive	imagining a likely future possibility (likely future)	**I hope that you enjoy** yourself tomorrow. **I hope that you are enjoying** yourself on vacation! **We hope that she doesn't make** the wrong decision.

- We can use *wish* to talk about ourselves or other people.

  I wish I had more friends. / I wish Sarah had more friends. / Sarah wishes her brother had more friends.
- We usually use *were* instead of *was* after *I wish* or *He/She wishes*.

  I wish I were better organized.
- We use *wish* + *could* to talk about something that we want to be different in the future. However, by using *could*, we express a belief that our wish probably won't come true.

  I wish I could treat myself to a vacation. (= I know that I won't be able to do this because I don't have the money, time, etc.)
- Although *hope* refers to the future, it is followed by a verb in the present tense. You can include the word *that*, but it is usually omitted.

  I hope (that) the snacks aren't too salty.
  We hope (that) the fast food restaurant is open tomorrow.
- We use the negative for the verb which **follows** *wish* or *hope*.

  I hope it doesn't rain tomorrow.
  NOT ~~I don't hope it rains.~~
  I wish I hadn't spent so much money.
  NOT ~~I don't wish I had spent so much money.~~

10.1 Third conditional; *Would have* + past participle

A Read the sentences and choose the option which is true.

1 He should have made a decision based on the facts.
 a He considered the facts. b He didn't consider the facts.
2 She could have avoided the other car if she'd stopped in time.
 a She avoided the other car. b She didn't avoid the other car.
3 If you had listened to me, you wouldn't have made a foolish decision.
 a You made a foolish decision. b You didn't make a foolish decision.
4 If David had gone to a smaller store, he would have felt less stressed.
 a David went to a small store. b David went to a big store.
5 You shouldn't have encouraged her to spend all that money!
 a She spent a lot of money. b She didn't spend a lot of money.
6 We wouldn't have bought this house if we'd known it was so noisy here.
 a We bought the house. b We didn't buy the house.

B Correct the mistakes in each sentence.

1 I shouldn't paid so much for this cell phone.
2 If our teacher gave us time to review, we would all have earned better grades.
3 Will the show have attracted more people if we had advertised it better?
4 I'm sorry – I would have listened to your advice.
5 If you have bought your shoes in the first store, you would have saved time!
6 Should we have count the sunk costs?
7 Would you had agreed to take part if you had known it was a trick?
8 I should realize that the watch was made of plastic!

➤ Go back to page 111.

C Choose the correct option.

The sneakers were fashionable, attractive and cheap, so I bought them. However, I [1]***shouldn't / wouldn't*** have been so easily influenced by the saleswoman. A few days later, I searched for that brand online and discovered that they were made by child workers! If I [2]***had known / would know*** that they were made by children, I would never [3]***buy / have bought*** them. In fact, I [4]***had avoided / would have avoided*** that store completely! If I [5]***would discover / had discovered*** the truth sooner, I would have complained to the store. And of course I [6]***hadn't encouraged / wouldn't have encouraged*** my friends to buy them either! It's really important that, as shoppers, we act responsibly. I've found an online group which persuades customers not to buy products like these. I joined it right away. If I [7]***had heard / heard*** about it sooner, I [8]***would / will*** have joined months ago!

➤ Go back to page 113.

10.2 Hopes and wishes

A Match the situations to the people's comments.

1 Brett's too short for the basketball team.
2 Dad is always losing his keys.
3 I don't know any of the answers.
4 Josh's drive to work takes 90 minutes.
5 I want to stop eating sugar completely.
6 Phoebe feels lonely.
7 Anna is really tired.

a 'I wish I didn't have to drive so far.'
b 'I wish I had studied more.'
c 'I wish I had more friends.'
d 'I wish I were taller.'
e 'I wish I hadn't stayed up all night.'
f 'I hope you achieve your goal.'
g 'I wish I wasn't so disorganized.'

B Choose the correct option.

1 I ***wish / hope*** to achieve everything on my to-do list.
2 Do you wish you ***don't give / hadn't given*** in to your cravings?
3 The children wish they ***could stay / stayed*** up late to watch the movie.
4 I wish I ***have / had*** more money to spend on clothes.
5 Kate wishes her husband ***is / were*** more focused on his career.
6 They wish they ***didn't live / couldn't live*** near a noisy shopping mall.
7 Jared ***wishes / hopes*** he could take a vacation.
8 I wish you ***didn't persuade / hadn't persuaded*** me to eat this burger – it's horrible!

C Complete the sentences with the correct form of the verb in parentheses.

1 I never have enough time. I wish there ________________ (*be*) more hours in the day!
2 I hope this snack ________________ (*not / be*) high in salt.
3 The children are full of energy. I wish they ________________ (*not / eat*) so many sugary snacks!
4 My children wish I ________________ (*not / work*) such long hours.
5 I hope Pam ________________ (*not / change*) her mind!
6 Alisha wants to buy a laptop but wishes she ________________ (*know*) more about them.
7 I wish my best friend ________________ (*be*) here to help me make the right choice!
8 She ________________ (*wish*) she could give up drinking sugary drinks but says it's very difficult.

➤ Go back to page 115.

Vocabulary Hub

6.2 Hobbies and free time activities

Complete the texts with the verb phrases in the box.

collect | escape from daily stress | get you out of the house | is a fan | is into | is relaxing | isn't my thing | joined a society | keeps you in shape | lost interest in | took up

My brother [1] ______________________ soccer. He [2] ______________________ of Liverpool Football Club and he goes to almost all their games. To be honest, soccer [3] ______________________, so I've only been to one game with him. I like to [4] ______________________ stamps. I've recently [5] ______________________ for that, and I'm going to my first meeting with the other members now. Who says stamp collecting doesn't [6] ______________________?!

Last year, I [7] ______________________ sailing as a hobby. I live in the city, and sailing is a great way to [8] ______________________. Being out on the lake with the wind in your hair [9] ______________________, and it [10] ______________________ too because you have to do a lot of physical work. I used to go to the gym, but I soon [11] ______________________ that. The running machines were too boring!

➤ Go back to page 66.

7.1 Phrasal verbs

Work in pairs. Match the underlined phrasal verbs (1–9) with the definitions (a–i).

1. I can't figure out what ingredients you've used here. What are they?
2. A: 'Maybe I'll start studying for my exams next week …'
   B: 'Don't put it off! Start today!'
3. We've eaten out every night this week. Let's stay in this evening and cook some food at home.
4. Sorry to let you down, but I can't come to your party.
5. I asked everybody to be quiet for a few minutes, but most people just kept on talking.
6. Can you turn the oven down to 150°C in ten minutes? If you leave it at 220°C for too long, the food will burn.
7. I don't mind cooking, but can you clean up afterward?
8. Can you put your phone away, please! It's really rude to check your messages while we're eating dinner!
9. Great job! Keep up the good work!

a. continue without stopping
b. take something that's in the wrong place and put it in the right place
c. continue at the same high level
d. make everything clean and neat again after making a mess
e. not go out
f. find the answer by thinking carefully
g. decide to do something later, not now
h. make something lower/colder/quieter
i. make somebody feel sad because you don't do something that you promised to do

➤ Go back to page 75.

7.1 Adjectives to describe food

A Complete the sentences with the adjectives in the box.

delicious disgusting filling mild savory sour

1 Our bakery sells a mix of sweet products, like cakes and fruit pies, and ______________ products, like bread and meat pies.

2 Do you prefer strong flavors or ______________ flavors?

3 Mmm … I love this meal. It's absolutely ______________!

4 I love ______________ food like lemons, grapefruit and pickled cabbage.

5 Ugh! How long has this milk been in the fridge? Two weeks? It tastes ______________!

6 This meal is great but it's very ______________ – I feel completely full already.

B Label the pictures with the adjectives in the box.

bitter raw rich spicy

1

____

2

____

3

____

4

____

➤ Go back to page 76.

8.2 Positive adjectives

Choose the best adjectives to complete the sentences.

1 A: My dog pressed six buttons in the right order!
B: That's so ***unique* / *impressive***!

2 I just want an umbrella that's ***incredible* / *practical*** – if it keeps me dry, I'm happy.

3 I read a ***fascinating* / *gorgeous*** article about the dangers of technology.

4 The party was ***sensible* / *unforgettable*** – I'll remember it for the rest of my life.

5 It's ***unique* / *incredible*** that people waste so much money on stupid gadgets!

6 It looks like a normal umbrella, but it contains very ***sophisticated* / *gorgeous*** electronics.

7 The CleverPet is ***sophisticated* / *suitable*** for small pets, like cats and dogs, but not large animals, like horses.

8 A: I lost my Oombrella. I forgot to take my phone with me.
B: Well, that wasn't very ***sensible* / *unique***, was it?

➤ Go back to page 90.

Vocabulary Hub

9.1 Verbal idioms

A Complete the sentences with the underlined verbal idioms in *The best (and the worst) of immersive theater*.

1. I can't really **tell** ________ ________ ________ immersive theater and interactive theater. Aren't they the same?
2. I tried to tell a joke, but it **fell** ________. Nobody understood it.
3. If you agree to help people all the time, they might **take** ________ ________ your kindness. You need to say 'no' more often.
4. Do you still have your old guitar, or did you **get** ________ ________ it?
5. Immersive plays usually **take** ________ in unusual locations.
6. They have a nice big yard, but they don't really **make** ________ ________ it.
7. Six actors **took** ________ ________ the play: four adults and two children.
8. I always write down the money I spend to help me **keep** ________ ________ my finances.
9. Everything is **going** ________ today! My computer stopped working and my car broke down!
10. If you don't **pay** ________ ________ your teacher, you won't learn very much.

B Complete the verbal idioms with the words in the box.

attention friends fun note sure true

1. I've always dreamed of being a chef, but I'm not sure my dream will ever **come** ________.
2. You shouldn't **make** ________ **of** other people's mistakes. They aren't funny at all.
3. When someone gives you good advice, always **take** ________ **of** what they say.
4. I **made** ________ **with** Alissa when we were at school, and we've liked each other ever since.
5. I didn't notice the sculpture in the corner. They should put it in the middle of the room to **draw** ________ **to** it!
6. I think I know the answer, but I need to check the internet to **make** ________.

➤ Go back to page 101.

10.2 Reflexive verbs

Complete the sentences with the correct reflexive pronouns. What do you think the reflexive verbs mean?

1. Can you all please behave ________! You're making too much noise!
2. Daisy bought ________ a box of chocolates this morning and ate every single one!
3. Where do you see ________ ten years from now, Hannah? Will you still be doing the same job?
4. Many people find it difficult to express ________ when they're speaking a foreign language. They know what they want to say, but they can't say it.
5. Look at that dog! It's having a good time playing in the water! It's really enjoying ________!
6. I want to do some exercise every day, but I don't trust ________. I'll probably give up after a week!
7. I need to go out for half an hour. Can you all amuse ________ while I'm gone?

➤ Go back to page 115.

6.2 Student A

Look at the table. Do you currently do these things? Complete the table so it is true for you. Then ask your partner questions and write down his/her answers.

	You		Your partner		
Activities	Yes/No?	How long?	Yes/No?	How long?	Other details
Use an app to study English					
Follow a celebrity on social media					
Regularly go to a favorite café					
Play a sport					
Collect something					
States					
Be a member of an online-only group					
Know someone from another country					
Have a desktop computer					
Have a car					

➤ Go back to page 67.

9.2 Student A

➤ Go back to page 105.

7.2 Students A and B

1 **a** about a week
   b 8–10 months
   c 4–5 days
   d 18–24 months
   e about 3 days
   f about 2 days

2 **a** False. You should only reheat food once.
   b True. After the best if used by date, the food may lose some taste or color, but it's probably still safe to eat for a little longer.
   c True. Rice sometimes contains very strong bacteria which aren't killed by cooking. So after cooking, put any leftover rice in the fridge and eat within 24 hours.

➤ Go back to page 80.

8.3 Student A

Use the pictures and notes to write instructions for making a paper airplane. Use sequencing phrases. Then read out your instructions so that Student B can make a paper airplane.

How to make a paper airplane

Put a piece of paper on the table.

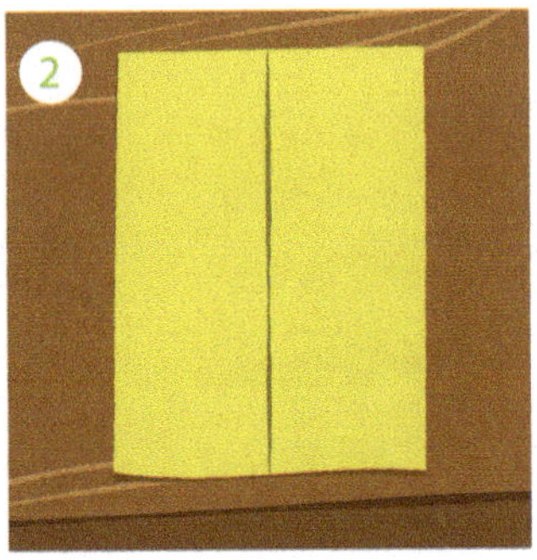

Fold the piece of paper in half lengthways, then unfold it.

Smooth it down.

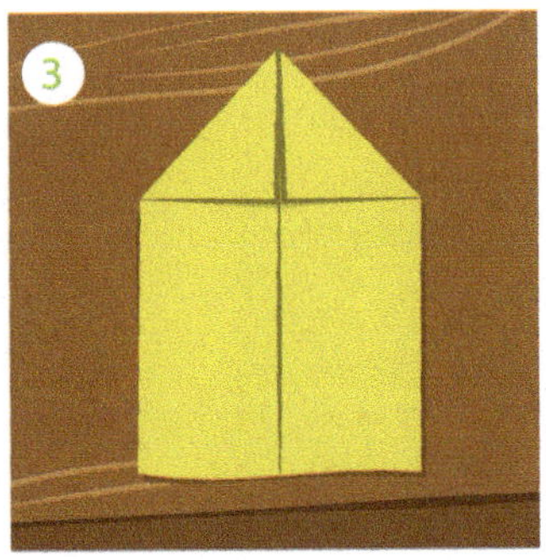

Form a point at the top of the paper.

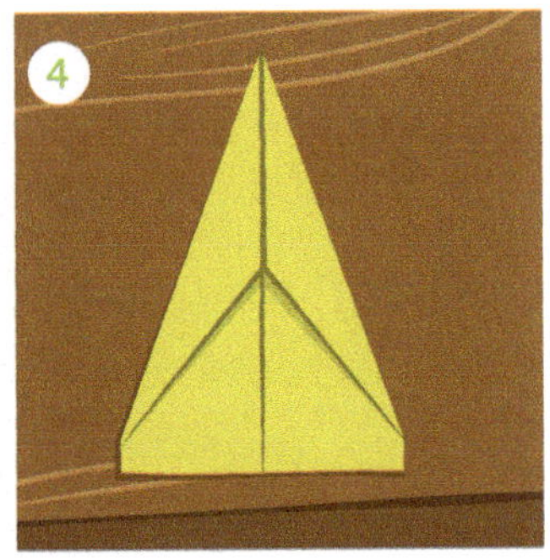

Fold the edges again.

Smooth down the edges with a ruler.

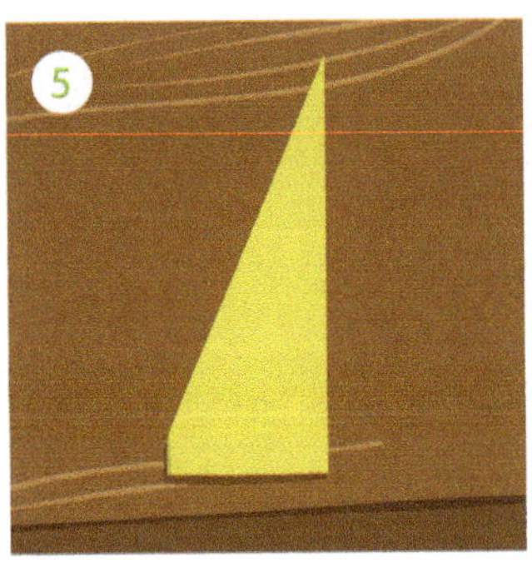

Fold the right side of the paper over the left side.

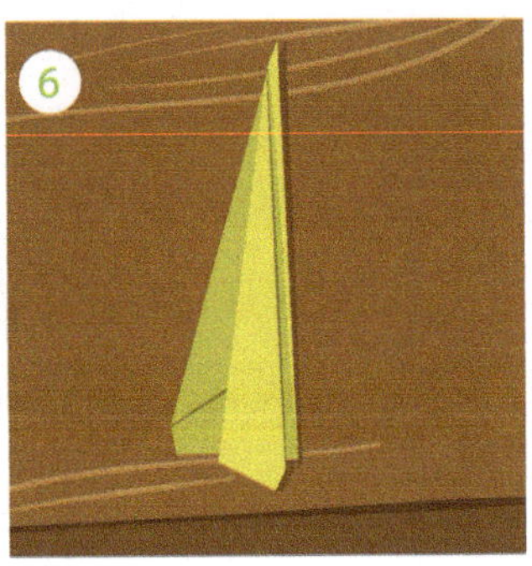

Create the wings.

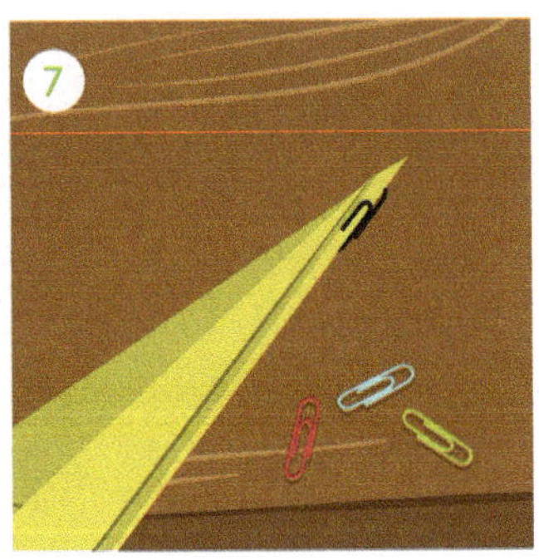

Attach a paperclip to the nose of the airplane – it will make it fly better.

Unfold the wings and you're ready for takeoff.

➤ Go back to page 95.

9.1 Student B

Proposal 2: Immersive theater

Costs (= money going out)		Income (= money coming in)
Building work: $100,000	Marketing: $150,000/year	Ticket sales: $1,500,000/year
Equipment: $150,000	Other costs (e.g. electricity): $150,000/year	Sponsorship: $500,000/year
Employees: $500,000/year		

- Sponsorship: Companies pay for their names/logos to be in the theater, on posters, etc.
- Ticket prices: $50–$100
- 80–100 tickets/performance; 400 performances/year (evenings and weekends only)
- No plans to help the community (e.g. free tickets for schools)

➤ Go back to page 99.

9.2 Student B

➤ Go back to page 105.

Communication Hub

9.1 Student C

Proposal 3: Modern art gallery

Costs (= money going out)	Income (= money coming in)
Building work and equipment: $150,000	Gift shop and snack bar: $150,000/year Sales of paintings, etc: $200,000–$500,000/year
Employees: $150,000/year	
Marketing: $50,000/year	
Other costs (e.g. electricity): $100,000/year	

- Two major exhibits each year (international artists, etc.)
- Smaller exhibits each month (local artists, etc.)
- Free entry for all people to all exhibits
- The gallery will take 40 percent of the sale price of any paintings (e.g. by local artists) that it sells.

➤ Go back to page 99.

8.3 Student B

Use the pictures and notes to write instructions for making a paper heart. Use sequencing phrases.
Then read out your instructions so that Student A can make a paper heart.

How to make a heart

You will need a square piece of paper.

Fold the piece of paper in half both ways, and unfold it so that you see the fold marks.

Turn the piece of paper around so that the point is at the top, and fold the top corner down to the middle.

Fold the bottom corner to the top.

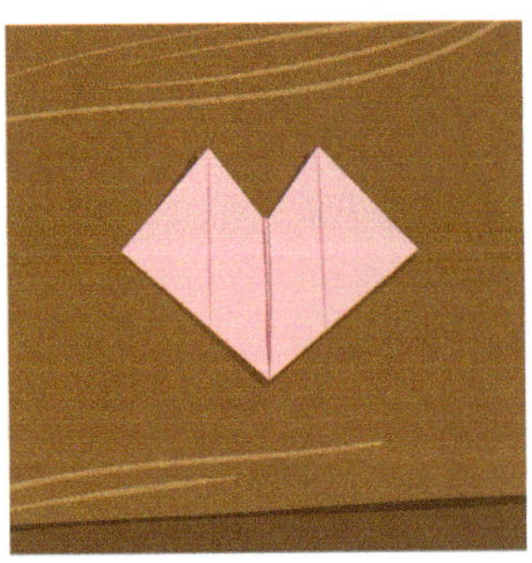

Fold the bottom edges to the middle.

Turn the paper over and fold the two top corners down.

Fold the corners down on both sides.

The heart is ready.

➤ Go back to page 95.

10.1 Students A and B

Take the quiz.

Psychology quiz

1 **a** Do we have more than 70 thoughts per day or fewer than 70?

b How many thoughts do we have each day?

2 You have paid for a weekend break in an expensive hotel. On the morning of your long journey, you feel sick and you just want to stay in bed. But it's too late to cancel your trip and get your money back. What do you do?

3 You're choosing a language school to help you pass an important exam. You know that 75 percent of School A's students passed the exam last year. You also know that 20 percent of School B's students failed the exam. Which school sounds better?

➤ Go back to page 110.

6.2 Student B

Look at the table. Do you currently do these things? Complete the table so it is true for you. Then ask your partner questions and write a note of his/her answers.

	You		Your partner		
Activities	**Yes/No?**	**How long?**	**Yes/No?**	**How long?**	**Other details**
Use an app to order food					
Write a blog					
Regularly go to a favorite movie theater					
Play a musical instrument					
Work for a company					
States					
Be a member of a club or society					
Know someone famous					
Have a laptop computer					
Have a pet					

➤ Go back to page 67.

6 Writing

Write an article for a magazine

W– introductory clauses

A Work in pairs. Read the magazine ad. Then look at the free time activities in the box. Which three do you think would be good subjects for an article? Why?

> Share your stories with *Life & Style*.
> In our Free time section, we're going to publish a new series of reader's articles, called *'Why everyone should ...!'*
> Send us your short articles about ideas for free time activities and hobbies – things that you think everyone should try doing at least once in their lifetime.

arts and crafts   playing soccer   skydiving
stamp collecting   stargazing (astronomy)
team video gaming

B Read *Why everyone should ... go stargazing!*. Put the sentences (a–f) in the order they are mentioned in the article (1–6).

a It is a good way to meet people. ___
b It is a simple hobby to start. ___
c Stargazing events at night are enjoyable. ___
d Cellular digital technology is useful. ___
e There is a place to go to use good equipment. ___
f You can join a club. ___

Why everyone should ... go stargazing!

Wow! That's all I can say as I look at the rings of Saturn, or see a shadow pass across the sun. I'll never regret taking up stargazing.

Besides the wonder of discovering the universe, the great thing about stargazing is that it is an easy hobby to take up. You only have to look up into the sky at night and you've already become a stargazer. The cool thing is that there are many cell phone apps to help you when you start, telling you exactly what you are looking at.

It is also easy to visit your local observatory. The wonderful thing about going there is that you can use powerful telescopes to see deep into the universe. You'll see the mountains of Mars, the moons of Jupiter and the stardust of the Milky Way.

A nice thing about stargazing is that it is actually very sociable. There are local societies all over the country, and enthusiasts frequently meet up for 'star parties'. They are like having a picnic at night and are a lot of fun. One thing to remember is that you should bring hot chocolate rather than juice – it's important to keep warm!

Everyone wants to put a little 'wow!' into their lives, and stargazing is a surprisingly simple, inexpensive and enjoyable way to do that. There's so much to discover in the universe, so isn't it time to start exploring?

C Read the tips on writing articles. Then look at the article again. Which tips did the writer follow? Give examples.

Top tips for writing a magazine article

1 In the introduction, clearly give the topic, and grab the reader's attention and interest.
2 Use a more relaxed and personal style than in a newspaper report.
3 Show your passion for the subject.
4 Give each paragraph a clear topic.
5 Use direct quotes from interviews.
6 Use humor.
7 In the conclusion, summarize the key points in the article.
8 Finish with a memorable sentence, giving the reader something to think about.

D Look at the box. Find and underline the introductory clauses in the highlighted sentences in the article.

Introductory clauses

We can begin a sentence with an introductory clause that provides, and draws attention to, the topic for the rest of the sentence.

E Work in pairs. Complete the sentences with information about a hobby, sport or activity that you do. Then compare your answers with a partner.

1 One good thing about __________ is that __________.
2 Something that I like about __________ is that __________.
3 A good reason to __________ is that __________.
4 One problem with __________ is that __________.
5 One thing to remember is that __________.

WRITING

A PREPARE You are going to write a short magazine article. Choose a hobby, sport or free time activity as the subject of your article. Why do you think everyone should try it?

B PLAN Write notes for your article. Read the tips in Exercise C again to help.

C WRITE Write an article (150–200 words).

D REVIEW Work in groups. Read the other students' articles. Which activities would you choose to do? Why?

Write a reply in an online discussion forum

comparing and recommending

A Work in pairs and discuss the questions.

1 Have you ever …
  a read an online discussion forum?
  b asked a question on an online discussion forum?
  c written a reply to somebody on an online discussion forum?

2 What kind of online discussion groups are you interested in? Use the ideas in the box and your own ideas.

current affairs   financial matters   food
health and fitness   music and movies   personal matters
product reviews and recommendations   travel

3 What's good about using these websites? What's bad about them?

B Read the forum post and the three replies. Which reply offers the best advice? What is the worst advice?

Message from Jo493

Hi. We have some relatives from another country coming to stay next week. I want to take them out to eat when they arrive after their long flight. I'm not sure whether to take them to an expensive restaurant or a fast-food joint.

I've asked them which they prefer, and they say they don't mind … but maybe they're just being polite. What do you recommend?

3 Comments

Reply from Miss Orange

It depends. Expensive restaurants serve better food, but of course they're much more expensive than fast-food joints. On the other hand, I like fast food because it's a lot faster than food from a restaurant. Why don't you ask them what they want to eat? Or how about cooking a meal for them instead?

Reply from hungry_al

I strongly recommend taking them for a good meal at an expensive restaurant. It'll make them feel special and welcome, and it should make an excellent first impression on them. They might be stressed after their flight, so they might want to go somewhere quiet and relaxing. You could always take them to a fast-food joint later during their stay with you – it's a nice thing to do with somebody you already know well. But for that first meeting, an expensive restaurant is far better.

Reply from Stewpot

I think you should take them for some fast food. After a long flight, they'll be tired and hungry, so they'll want to eat as quickly as possible. Another thing to remember is that your visitors might not feel very fresh and clean after their flight, and they may not have suitable clothes for a fancy restaurant. So you'll have to take them home first so they can change their clothes … and that could take hours. It's much quicker and easier if you take them for some simple food at a fast-food joint. After all, you can always take them to your favorite restaurant the next day. Good luck!

C Read again. Which reply or replies …

1 started with a clear recommendation?
2 ended with a clear recommendation?
3 introduced a third option?
4 thought about how the visitors will feel after their trip?
5 missed some important information in the original message?
6 gave reasons to explain why their recommendation is better?
7 suggested a way of using both options?

D Look at the box. Choose *Do* or *Don't* for each rule.

Comparing and recommending

1 **Do / Don't** start with a clear recommendation. (I think you should …; I strongly recommend …)
2 **Do / Don't** say it depends. The writer is asking you for a recommendation, so don't make their decision more complicated.
3 **Do / Don't** use comparatives to show why your option is better. (It's much quicker and easier …)
4 **Do / Don't** just talk about what you prefer.
5 **Do / Don't** show that you have thought about the people in the situation. (They might be stressed after their flight, so …)
6 **Do / Don't** give reasons for your recommendation.
7 **Do / Don't** add extra suggestions.
8 **Do / Don't** end with a clear recommendation. (… is far better.)

WRITING

A PLAN Read the forum post. What are the two options? Write notes on some arguments for and against each option.

I want to organize a dinner party for about 20 people from work and their families. I like the idea of a pot luck dinner party, but I've heard they don't always work well. Maybe I should just cook all the food myself. What do you recommend?

B WRITE Which option will you recommend? Write your reply (100–150 words).

C REVIEW Work in groups. Read each other's replies. Did everyone follow all the rules in the skills box? Who wrote the best recommendation?

8 Writing

Write a biography

W using linking words to show contrast

A SPEAK Work in pairs. Read the short biography *Sal Khan, founder of the Khan Academy.*

1 Who is Sal Khan?
2 What are the main events in his life?
3 How innovative is he? Why?

Sal Khan, founder of the Khan Academy

1 Sal Khan is one of the most innovative people in education today. The Khan Academy, which he started in 2006, makes free online videos to teach people around the world about math, science and many other things.

2 Sal was born near New Orleans, US, in 1976. After college, he found a well-paid job in finance. However, he soon realized there was more to life than money.

3 Sal's life changed in 2004, when he started giving math lessons to members of his family. To save time, he decided to record his lessons and post them on YouTube. Despite the simple quality of the videos, they soon became popular around the world. Suddenly, he was teaching millions of people and making a real difference to their lives.

4 Although Sal didn't invent video-based learning, he helped make it popular and successful. His main innovation was to give everything away for free. As a result, he can really help those people who need it.

5 Sal's story teaches us that we don't need to be an inventor to be innovative, and we don't need to be powerful to change the world. In fact, we just need to do something we love. Hopefully, we can help other people along the way.

B Read again. Are the sentences true (T) or false (F)? Correct the false sentences.

1 You can only watch the videos in the US. ___
2 Sal's first job was as a teacher. ___
3 He made videos because he wanted to be famous. ___
4 Sal was the first person to teach using YouTube videos. ___
5 The writer thinks that Sal loves his work. ___

C A good biography usually has five sections. Match the sections (1–5) with the explanations (a-e). Use the biography of Sal Khan to help you.

1 introduction
2 backstory
3 turning point
4 impact
5 conclusion

a the story of the person's early life: family, education, first jobs, etc.
b why the person is special; how they changed the world
c lessons for our own lives
d who you are writing about and that person's biggest achievements
e something happened that changed the person's life

D Look at the box. Add an example of each linking word from Sal Khan's biography.

Using linking words to show contrast

We use linking words (*although, despite, however*) to link two different or contrasting ideas, one of which is unexpected, surprising or seems to be contradictory.

although **+ subject + verb**

- ***Although*** *Sal Khan isn't an inventor, he's very innovative.*
- *Sal Khan is very innovative,* ***although*** *he isn't an inventor.*

1 ______________________________

despite **+ noun**

2 ______________________________

despite **+ (*not*) + verb + *-ing***

- ***Despite*** *not being an inventor, Sal Khan is very innovative.*

despite the fact that **+ subject + verb**

- ***Despite the fact that*** *he isn't an inventor, Sal Khan is very innovative.*

however

- *Sal Khan isn't an inventor.* ***However,*** *he's very innovative.*
- *Sal Khan is very innovative;* ***however,*** *he isn't an inventor.*

3 ______________________________

E Complete the sentences with the correct linking words.

1 ______________ the fact that he had no experience as an engineer, he solved an extremely difficult engineering problem.
2 Nobody was interested in her ideas at first, ______________ they became a lot more popular later.
3 Her invention was gorgeous and extremely innovative. ______________, it was far too expensive at first.
4 She ended up changing the world ______________ some very serious challenges at the beginning.
5 ______________ he was only 14 at the time, he managed to win the design competition.

WRITING

A PREPARE You are going to write a short biography of a famous innovator or an innovative friend or family member.

B PLAN Use the five-section plan in Exercise C to help you.

C WRITE Write your biography (about 200 words). Try to use linking words to show contrasting ideas. Use the skills box to help you. Check your grammar and spelling.

D REVIEW Work in groups. Read the other students' biographies. Which biography is about the most innovative person?

using colons to introduce explanations

A Look at the pictures and read the reviews. Which event was better, the exhibit or the concert?

Robert Gonsalves exhibit at the TACA

One of my favorite artists is Robert Gonsalves (1959–2017). I fell in love with his incredible paintings years ago, so I was delighted to visit an exhibit of his work last month at the Toronto Academy of Contemporary Art.

His paintings show beautiful scenes with a twist: they all show two different worlds coming together. This means you can enjoy the paintings on two levels: first as objects of beauty, and then as amazing ideas to help you see the world differently.

However, I visited the exhibit on a Saturday afternoon, when it was extremely crowded. At times, it was difficult to get close to the paintings. Also, the space felt too small for so many paintings. If there were only one painting on each wall, it would create a much more powerful impression.

Overall, I would strongly recommend the exhibit, but you should go when it is less crowded.

Mel Montuno in concert at the City Arena

Last night I attended a concert by Mel Montuno, one of today's most exciting young musicians.

I became a fan of Mel's music two years ago, when I saw her performing live for an audience of 30. Now she is an international star – she usually has audiences of 10,000!

Although Mel is still an incredible songwriter with a beautiful voice, I definitely preferred her before she was famous. Last night's concert felt 'too big': she looked uncomfortable with such a large audience and hardly interacted with her fans at all.

More seriously, the music was too loud and the lights were painfully bright. After half an hour, I had to leave, to give my ears and eyes a break!

Mel Montuno is currently on an eight-city tour of the country. If you like huge concerts, you might want to buy a ticket. But if, like me, you prefer calm, beautiful music, I recommend buying Mel's new CD, *My Jazz Age*, instead.

B Read again and answer the questions.

1. Why did the writer decide to go to the exhibit/concert?
2. What did the writer like?
3. What wasn't so good?
4. What does the writer recommend? Why?

C What is the purpose of the paragraphs in each review? How are the two reviews similar? How are they different?

D Read the advice about writing reviews. Find examples of each piece of advice in the reviews.

1. Add a personal touch to describe how you felt.
2. Include practical information.
3. Don't be too negative – write about how you would do things differently or why people might not mind the problems.
4. Avoid repeating words like *beautiful* or *amazing*. Try to include a range of words instead.
5. Always end with a clear recommendation for your readers.

E Look at the box. Find three colons in the reviews. Underline the explanations after each colon. Circle the key phrase before each colon.

Using colons to introduce explanations

We can use colons (:) to join two sentences together and show how they are connected. The information after the colon provides an explanation for the key phrase before the colon.

F Match the beginnings of the review writers' sentences (1–3) with the endings (a–c).

1. There were three problems with the restaurant:
2. My recommendation couldn't be clearer:
3. When I arrived at the festival, I got an unpleasant surprise:

a. go and buy tickets for this concert immediately.
b. the food was bad, the service was slow and the prices were too high.
c. half of the musicians had canceled their live shows because of the bad weather.

WRITING

A PREPARE You are going to write a review of an art event. Write about a real event that you attended or invent one.

B PLAN Write notes. Think about:

1. What was good about the event?
2. What would you improve? How?
3. Would you recommend the event to other people?

C WRITE Write your review (150–200 words).

D REVIEW Work in groups. Read some of your classmates' reviews. Which events would you like to attend?

W— writing a report

A Work in pairs and discuss the questions.

1. Why do people write reports? What are some situations where non-business people write reports?
2. Why do people read reports? What information do they need?

B Read the *Report on charity auction* and answer the questions.

1. Why has the writer written the report?
2. What went well with the auction? What went wrong?
3. What did the writer learn from the experience?

REPORT ON CHARITY AUCTION

Summary:
On December 15, we held a charity auction to raise money for the local hospital. The auction raised less money than expected. This report explores what we did wrong.

Background:
We asked 24 local celebrities (e.g. sportspeople, TV presenters) to donate gifts for our auction. We received 55 gifts, including many valuable items (e.g. a signed soccer ball, a beautiful painting). We expected to raise around $5,000. 720 people attended our auction event. The auction only raised $322. Many of the items were not sold.

Analysis:
1. **Paradox of choice:** There were too many items, so people could not decide. If we had limited the auction to around ten items, we would probably have made more money.
2. **Hook numbers:** We wanted to attract large numbers of people to the auction, so in our marketing materials, we showed pictures of the best items with low starting prices, e.g. $2 for the signed soccer ball. We shouldn't have done this because it encouraged people to make offers of a few dollars, not hundreds of dollars.

Recommendations:
- For future auctions, limit the number of items to around ten.
- In marketing materials, show the value of the items (e.g. *Worth over $500*) rather than the starting price.

Glossary

auction (n) a public occasion when things are sold to the people who offer the most money for them
donate (v) to give something such as money or goods to an organization, especially to a school, hospital, political party or charity

C Look at the box. Match the features of a report (1–8) with the explanations (a–h). Find examples in the report.

Writing a report

A report describes a past event or a present situation and ends with recommendations for the future.

1. title
2. summary
3. headings
4. bullet points
5. numbered lists
6. full forms
7. facts and figures
8. examples

a. Use these small black circles to make it easier to read lists of items.
b. Your report should include dates, names, numbers, etc.
c. In the first paragraph, say briefly what happened and why you've written the report.
d. The reader can see immediately what the report is about.
e. You can use these to show that the order of items in a list is important.
f. Use words like *Analysis* and *Recommendations* to show you're starting a new section.
g. Include these to explain important points. You can put them in parentheses: (e.g. …).
h. Reports are usually fairly formal, so it's best to write separate words (e.g. *do not*) instead of contractions (e.g. *don't*).

D Find examples of the third conditional and *would have* or *should have done* in the report. Which section are they in? Why?

WRITING

A PREPARE You are going to write a short report about an event where some things could have been better. Think about:

- will you write about a real event or will you invent one?
- what event will you describe? Something from your work or studies? An accident that you had?
- who will read your report? Why?

B PLAN Write notes under these headings:

- Background: What happened?
- Analysis: What went wrong? Why?
- Recommendations: What should happen differently in the future?

C WRITE Write your report. Remember to use headings, bullet points or numbered lists. When you finish writing the three main sections, write a short summary at the beginning.

D REVIEW Work in groups. Read some of your groups' reports. Do you agree with their recommendations?

UNIT 6

Lesson 6.1, Listening, Exercise B

6.1 Soccer, // basketball, // golf, // tennis // – four of the world's most popular sports. / They are played by millions / and watched by millions more, / and all four / are in the greatest festival of sports, // the Olympic Games.

However, // there is one sport / that is just as popular as those, / but it still hasn't been accepted in the Olympics, / and indeed, // many people say / that it is not even a sport. / What sport am I talking about? // eSports. / Yes, // electronic sports, / or competitive video gaming.

Now, I guess many of you think video games are just something people play at home or on their phones. In fact, they are played in the same way as any other sport, with teams competing against each other in large venues and stadiums, in front of thousands of paying spectators, and with millions more watching online.

Even if you already know how massive eSports are, maybe many of you think gaming is not actually a sport. But I hope to persuade you that video gaming has all the features that we see in other sports.

First of all, it is clearly competitive. Players and teams compete in national and international tournaments, with a goal to win the final, lift the trophy and become the champions. The will to win is a key part of video gaming.

Also, playing video games requires incredible mental strength and skill. You need to focus for long periods of time and the games are very fast. eSports demand smart thinking, quick decision-making and great communication between team members, just like traditional team sports.

Of course, some people argue that video gaming is not a real sport because it doesn't require physical strength. Now, I accept it isn't the same as soccer or football, for example, but, because the games are long and demanding, professional gamers have to be very fit. If your fitness levels are poor, so is your ability to concentrate. This is why the managers and coaches of professional teams make sure their players spend time training in the gym and have a healthy diet. That all sounds like a sport to me.

So, have I changed your mind yet? Do you now feel that eSports should be in the Olympics? If not, remember that when they choose new sports for the games, they are looking for ones that are popular and have strong youth appeal. That sounds like eSports to me. Online eSports platforms have hundreds of millions of users every week. While the numbers of people playing and watching traditional sports are declining, they are rapidly increasing for eSports, and most of those people are young people.

So, eSports are physically and mentally demanding. They attract young people like no other sport. They are popular all over the world, and, of course, anyone can take part. They have already become a professional success story, with famous top players, great teams, and enthusiastic fans.

Video gaming is not a sport of the future; it is a sport of today, and so, eSports should, undoubtedly, be in the Olympic Games. Now, please excuse me, but I have a game to go and play. Thank you.

Lesson 6.1, Listening, Exercise D

6.2 In fact, they are played in the same way as any other sport, with teams competing against each other in large venues and stadiums, in front of thousands of spectators, and with millions more watching online.

Lesson 6.2, Listening, Exercise B

6.5 **RP = Radio Presenter S1 = Speaker 1 S2 = Speaker 2 S3 = Speaker 3 S4 = Speaker 4 S5 = Speaker 5**

RP: Hobbies. Interests. Pastimes. They're something more than watching TV, and something different from playing a sport. I'm Gavin Ross, and in this week's *Human Behavior*, we're asking you, the public, about what you like doing in your free time. What hobbies do you have? How long have you been doing them? Why do you have them? Let's hear from some of our listeners out on the streets in Boston today.

S1: I'm really into classic or vintage cars. I've been buying them since I was 18, when I first learned to drive and got my first one, a small 1960s sports car. Obviously, it isn't exactly a cheap hobby, what with buying and then repairing them. It means I don't go on expensive vacations like my friends, but I'm not going to give it up. I've just bought an old Mini, so I'll start working on that tomorrow.

S2: Arts and crafts are my thing – jewelry making, painting, woodwork. I've had this interest since I was a child. For the last six months, I've been going to pottery classes. In fact, I've been working in the studio this afternoon – that's why my hands are so dirty. As a hobby, it's relaxing and a great escape from daily stress, and, you know, it makes time fly – a sure sign I'm enjoying myself.

S3: I don't really have a hobby, but my husband is an enthusiastic cyclist. Actually, I think that cycling is an obsession for him, rather than a hobby. If he isn't out on a ride, he's cleaning the thing, or checking out the latest accessories online. He's been doing it since his teens, so I knew what I was getting when I married him. It isn't really my thing, so I leave him to it; it seems to keep him in shape and happy.

S4: I don't know if you can call this a hobby, but I spend most of my time following Danny CJ, the singer – I'm a massive fan. I've been a member of his fan club for a long time, I've been to a lot of his concerts and I collect everything I can about him: all the music, pictures, posters, calendars. It's great following him on social media, too. He even replied to one of my tweets once. Whenever he comes to Boston, my friends and I all hang out outside his hotel. He's in there now – we've been waiting here all day, but we haven't seen him yet. Hold on, is that him? Danny! Danny! Over here!

S5: Do I have a hobby? Well, you might say my hobby is having hobbies. I tend to get really into something, like, at first, I get really obsessed with it, but then I soon lose interest. I don't know why. I've always been like this. Recently, I've been getting into bird watching – I've bought all the kits and a bunch of books, and I've joined two local societies. No idea how long this will last though. I might start cooking classes soon, or take up sailing. Anything that gets me out of the house.

RP: Those are just some of the people I've met while making this show, and I'd like to hear from even more of you. Visit our show's website to see how you can take part in this series of *Human Behavior*. The address is www.radiotalk.nett/humanbehavior …

UNIT 7

Lesson 7.1, Listening, Exercise C

7.2 **V = Vicky C = Charlie T = Tina M = Markus**

V: Charlie! You're here at last!

C: Hi, Vicky. Sorry I'm a little late.

V: No problem. You're only … 20 minutes late. Welcome to pot luck night.

C: Thanks. Am I the last person here?

V: No, actually, there's only one other person so far. He arrived half an hour early!

C: Oh, that must be Felipe, right? He's always early.

V: True. But it was good because he helped me make my dish: a cheese and chilli salad.

C: Ah … I'm allergic to dairy products. Oh, well. Never mind.

V: Hmm. Wow … those look delicious, Charlie. What are they?

C: Spicy buffalo wings. They're a traditional dish from New York made with a hot sticky sauce.

V: Wow. That's … different.

C: Yes, that's what I thought. Uh … can I heat them up in the oven? They just need 15 minutes.

V: Sure, but you'll have to wait ten minutes. I'm heating up Felipe's dish right now.

C: OK, no problem.

V: Great. Let me take your dish. Go and join Felipe – he's waiting in the backyard.

C: OK, thanks.

V: Aha … Tina. Welcome to pot luck night!

T: Thanks. Is everyone else here already?

V: No, not yet. But Felipe's here, and Charlie.

T: Those look nice. What are they?

V: Buffalo wings. Charlie brought them. Hmm … I've never eaten buffalo meat before. I wonder what it tastes like.

T: Hang on … that can't be right. They can't be buffalo wings. Buffaloes don't have wings!

V: No, you're right. But they're definitely wings. They could be chicken or something like that.

T: Aha … yes. Isn't there a city called Buffalo in New York? The name must come from the city, not the animal.

V: Good thinking. Anyway, what have you brought?

T: It's my own recipe. It's called cheesy chicken pasta surprise.

V: Oh, right. What's the surprise?

T: Ah … you'll have to wait and see. Can I just heat it up in the oven?

V: Well, uh … you'll have to wait for Charlie's dish … and Felipe's dish. It's chicken curry in a creamy sauce.

T: Oh, yes, so that's what smells so good. I love hot, spicy food.

V: Great. So let me take your dish to the kitchen. Go and join the others out in the backyard.

V: Markus! Great to see you. Come on in.

M: Thanks. I'm so sorry I'm late … again! You must think I'm so disorganized!

V: No, don't worry. Most of the others have just arrived, too. So … what have you brought?

M: Cream of chicken soup. I hope that's OK.

V: Uh … yeah, I hope so, too. But I don't have any soup bowls, so it might be a little difficult. I suppose we could drink it from cups. Uh … do I need to heat it up?

M: No, don't worry. I heated it up before I left. That looks great. What is it?

V: It's Tina's cheesy chicken pasta surprise.

M: Ah. It smells great, but … what are those red things?

V: They look like they might be chilies.

M: Oh, I hope not! I hate spicy food.

V: Well, they might not be chilies. They may be red peppers or something.

M: No, they're definitely chilies. Oh, well – hopefully there are some other dishes that I can eat.

V: Uh … you may have a problem there. We also have Felipe's spicy chicken curry and Charlie's spicy chicken wings.

M: Oh, no! Well, at least I have my chicken soup. And it means there will be more food for you.

V: Uh … not really. I don't like chicken.

Lesson 7.2, Listening, Exercise B

7.5 **H = Host MT = Mrs. Taylor Mr.T = Mr. Taylor P = Philip A = Alison**

H: Hello and welcome to *The Food Fad Show*. Today, we're talking about food waste. Did you know that globally, we waste a huge amount of the food we produce. The average person, just one person, wastes $200 of food every year. Can you believe that? $200!

H: In the studio today we have the Taylor family. A year ago, they decided to reduce the amount of food they waste every year by 50 percent. Tell us more, Mrs. Taylor.

MT: Well, I've been interested in food waste for a long time. But the more I researched the topic, the more I realized that we aren't just throwing away food; we're also throwing away hundreds of dollars per year – enough to pay for a nice family vacation. That's when I decided we needed to cut our own waste dramatically.

H: OK, so what have you done to save money?

MT: Let me give you an example. Ugly carrots taste just as good as beautiful carrots, but in our local grocery store, they cost less than half as much. As far as I'm concerned, the uglier, the better! Also, my grocery store always lowers the price of meat or dairy products that are getting close to their best if used by date. So it's usually possible to buy food a lot more cheaply by checking those dates carefully. As long as you eat the food soon after buying it, it's completely safe.

H: Right. So it's all about money, then, Mr. Taylor?

Mr.T: No, not really. Food production has a massive impact on the environment: first to produce the food and distribute it, and then to get rid of any waste. I always thought the best way to save the planet was to reduce the amount of garbage we throw away and to reuse and recycle as much as possible. But in fact, the food itself has a much greater impact than the packaging it comes in. For example, throwing away a head of lettuce harms our planet 100 times more than throwing away the plastic bag.

H: Really? That's amazing. Why?

Mr.T: Well, just think of all the water needed to grow it, the electricity to keep the greenhouse at just the right temperature, and then the environmental cost of keeping it fresh all the way from the farm to your fridge. It all adds up!

H: Wow! I'd never thought of that!

Mr.T: Here's another example. It takes 100 buckets of water to bake one loaf of bread. A hundred! Think about that the next time you throw away some one-day-old bread. If we could end all food waste around the world, it would be like taking one quarter of the world's cars off the roads. As far as I'm concerned, the less food we throw away, the better.

H: OK, so what have you done to cut down on food waste? Alison?

A: Yes, well, before our experiment, Mom or Dad always served up a large plate of food for each of us, but it was usually too much for me. So half of it always went in the garbage can. These days, we all help ourselves to food from a serving dish in the middle of the table. It's great because now we only take what we want – and we eat everything on our plates. It's much better because the less we cook, the less we waste.

H: OK, great. And what about leftovers?

A: When we started off, we had a rule that we had to eat yesterday's leftovers before any fresh food. But it was awful, so we stopped it. I mean, yesterday's leftovers are disgusting! Who wants to eat those? But now we use those leftovers to make soup or a stew. It's still a little strange, but the longer we do it, the more normal it feels.

H: Yes, I'm sure. OK, and what about Philip? Can I ask you a question or are you too busy playing on your phone?

P: Don't worry – I'm not playing. I wanted to show you a cool cell phone app. It helps us keep track of exactly what food we have in the house – and when that food will go bad.

H: Oh, OK. Sorry. So … how does it work?

P: Well, you need to type in all the numbers whenever you buy – or eat – anything. Some people might find that to be a waste of time, but I like that sort of thing. Of course, you don't need to count every single potato, for example, but the more carefully you count things, the more accurate your results will be. It's really fascinating when you study the numbers. Now, whenever we're in the grocery store, we can check what we need and what we don't. The app also sends us a notification when something is getting close to its best if used by date. That's really useful.

H: Yes, I'm sure.

P: And it even suggests delicious meal ideas to use up the ingredients we have, instead of buying new ones all the time. I never enjoyed cooking before, but thanks to the app, it's a lot more fun. And best of all, the app tells us exactly how much money we're saving every day.

H: Oh, yes. Tell us about the money, Mrs. Taylor.

MT: Well, so far, it's been a great success. According to Philip's app, we've managed to save $730 in food bills alone over the past year. And guess what? We're going on vacation next week to celebrate our excellent achievement.

H: Wow! Congratulations!

UNIT 8

Lesson 8.1, Listening, Exercise B

8.3 **C = Caroline T = Toby**

C: Hey, Toby. Do you want some coffee?

T: No, thanks. I'm in a hurry. I need to go to the library to work on my project for college.

C: Really? What's the project?

T: We have to invent 'something that will make a difference to people's lives'. But I'm terrible at coming up with ideas. They didn't teach us how to be creative in school when I was younger! But you, you're so creative. I mean, you write amazing stories; you design beautiful clothes. How do you do it?

C: Well, you can actually learn to use your imagination better. I've read a lot of books about creativity, and I've learned some great techniques from them.

T: Really? Can you give me an example?

C: Well, whenever I feel like I have too much work, I always stop working for an hour or so.

T: But I don't have time to stop. I'm really busy!

C: I always thought the same. But when I tried it, I found that a break actually boosted my creativity. When I'm relaxed, I have lots more creative ideas, and I'm much more productive after a break – I get more work done in less time. Tell me, how do you fill your time in the evenings?

T: Uh, I usually just watch TV or play games on my phone. I'm too tired to do anything else.

C: Aha. So that's what's blocking your creativity: you're filling your brain with information all the time. You need to unplug completely. Instead of watching TV, go for a run. You need to let your mind wander freely.

T: OK, I guess I can watch less TV. But I hate running!

C: Well, it doesn't have to be running. You could go dancing or swimming, or get some other type of physical exercise. They're all good for generating new ideas.

T: OK. I love swimming, so I guess I could go to the swimming pool once a week.

C: Great. Swimming's actually perfect because the water is blue.

T: Uh, sorry? What does that have to do with creativity?

C: Well, I read recently that the color blue makes us more creative. Whenever I need to think outside the box, I go to the beach and look at the sky and the ocean. It always helps.

T: OK, but it doesn't really help me with my project. I need to start work on it right now. I'm actually getting stressed about it.

C: Well, maybe that's the problem: you're letting your emotions block your creativity. You should look at a problem from the outside, to take away the emotions. Then it's much easier to find a solution. That's why it's easier to solve other people's problems than your own – because you can focus on the problems, not the emotions.

T: OK, but …

C: So another good technique is to discuss your ideas with other people – and listen to what they say. The best solutions usually come from group discussions and brainstorming sessions. And if there's nobody you can talk to, you can imagine having a conversation with a friend. Look at the problem through someone else's eyes.

T: OK, yes, I know what you mean. But what about my project? I need to come up with an invention right now. But I don't have any ideas at all. My mind's gone blank!

C: Well, there's one last trick I usually use when I really have no ideas. I call it the alphabet technique. OK, so tell me three letters of the alphabet.

T: Uh, W, G and P.

C: Perfect. So your invention needs to solve a problem, and that problem needs to start with your first letter, W.

T: Water? It isn't really a problem, is it?

C: Well, let's use your second letter to help us. What was it?

T: G for – grass. Hmm, water, grass. Aha, maybe the invention could be a better way of watering the grass in people's yards when they're away on vacation. I mean, just pouring water onto the grass all day and all night is really wasteful. But what's the solution?

C: I don't know. But it needs to start with your third letter, which was …?

T: P – for plastic bottles. Aha, I could use old plastic bottles, filled with water. Then I could make tiny holes in the bottles, so the water comes out really slowly, over a week or two.

C: Sounds good!

T: Hmm. I need to think about this carefully. OK, I'm going for a long walk along the beach to figure out the details. See you later.

C: OK. Call me if you need any help! Good luck!

Lesson 8.2, Listening, Exercises B and C

8.4 **L = Leo T = Teresa**

L: Hello, and welcome to this week's *Must-have Gadgets* podcast. I'm Leo Kovalski.

T: And I'm Teresa Martinez. Now, earlier this week I went to the International Gadget Show, where I saw some really amazing gadgets. And I've brought two along today to show you, Leo.

L: Sounds great. So what do you have for us?

T: Well, let's start with a very sensible invention: the Oombrella. What do you think, Leo?

L: Uh … it just looks like a normal umbrella. I mean, the design is gorgeous, really nice, but … it isn't exactly innovative, is it?

T: Oh! But this Oombrella is unique. It's the world's first umbrella that's connected to the internet.

L: What? Why on earth do I need an umbrella that connects to the internet?

T: Well, did you bring an umbrella to work today?

L: No, unfortunately. I forgot to check the weather forecast, so I didn't know it was going to rain.

T: Aha. Well, you can borrow my Oombrella today. It'll check the weather forecast for you. If the forecast says it's going to rain later, Oombrella will send a message to your cell phone.

L: OK, but why do I need a special umbrella just to send weather forecasts to my phone?

T: Well, the Oombrella is especially suitable for forgetful people, like you, who forget to check the weather forecast on their phones.

L: Yes, well, I am a fairly forgetful person. But what do forgetful people do all the time? They leave their umbrellas behind in cafés, or on the bus! What if I lose your Oombrella tonight?

T: Well, if you leave it behind, you'll get a message on your phone. They call it the unforgettable umbrella because you can't forget it.

L: OK, yes, that is pretty practical, I suppose.

T: Yes. And the Oombrella also has lots of sophisticated electronics: if you go for a long walk in the rain tonight, the app will send you a weather report when you get home. So you can read all about the weather during your walk.

L: Hmm … I'm not sure I need an Oombrella. I never go for a walk unless the sun's shining. The big question for me is: will it keep me dry if there's a storm tomorrow morning when I'm coming to work?

T: Absolutely! It's made of super-strong materials, so it won't break. You'll be able to use it for years.

L: Really? Well that is impressive. My umbrellas always break after five minutes in a storm. So if this Oombrella lasts for years, I'll be very happy.

T: Well, I only said you could borrow mine. I'd like to have it back tomorrow.

L: Oh, yes, of course. So … what else do you have?

T: Well, the second gadget is called CleverPet. It's a food bowl for dogs and cats.

L: Great. And don't tell me … it's connected to the internet, right?

T: Yes! How did you guess? Do you have any pets, Leo?

L: Yes, I have a dog named Henry.

T: And what does Henry do all day, while you're at work?

L: Uh … not much. He sleeps most of the day, but sometimes he chews the furniture in my apartment.

T: Well, that's because he's bored. Of course he chews your furniture if he has nothing else to do all day.

L: OK. And what does this have to do with your incredible internet-connected dog food bowl?

T: Well, it isn't just a bowl. It's a puzzle.

L: A puzzle? For dogs?

T: Yes. There are three buttons with lights. When a light flashes, the dog has to press a button. If he presses the right button, the light goes on again and he wins something to eat.

L: OK.

T: Then, over the next few days, weeks, even years, the puzzles get more and more difficult. The dog has to remember lots of information and press the buttons in the right order.

L: Oh, right. And, uh, do dogs enjoy puzzles?

T: Absolutely! They love them. It keeps them busy for hours, which means they never get bored. And if they don't get bored, they don't chew the furniture.

L: Well, I must admit, it sounds fascinating.

T: It is. And it really helps pets stay active. Scientists have shown that pets stay healthier and they live longer if they keep busy. You should definitely get one for Henry.

L: Yes, I think I might!

T: Great.

L: OK, so that's all from today's podcast. We'll be back next time with more must-have gadgets. Thanks for listening.

UNIT 9

Lesson 9.1, Listening, Exercise B

9.1 **C = Chair L = Leon V = Violet F = Florian**

C: Welcome to the final of the Warehouse Project competition. Now, we received hundreds of excellent ideas, but there can only be one winner. Today, the three finalists are here to present their proposals before the public vote later this evening. But for now, let's hear from the first finalist, Leon MacGregor.

L: Thank you. I'd like to present my proposal to turn the warehouse into a community music center, with modern recording studios, rehearsal rooms and a performance area for live concerts. If the proposal is successful, people will be able to use the center free of charge. I believe music can make a big difference to our community, especially for older people who have retired from work. If we open a community music center, it will change thousands of people's lives, by giving them opportunities to go out, meet new people and learn new skills. Won't that be wonderful for our city?

My dream is for the people of this city to join music classes with professional musicians, to learn how to sing or to play a musical instrument. They'll work together to form bands, orchestras and choirs. They'll have the space and equipment they need to rehearse and create new music. And they'll be able to perform live in front of an audience. If you share my dream, vote for my proposal to help it come true. Music … for the community.

C: Thank you, Leon. Our next finalist is Violet Spring.

V: Thank you. As an actor, I love the theater. And I'm not alone – tens of thousands of people all over the country visit the theater every day. But not in this city. Since the Grand Theater closed down ten years ago, theater-lovers have had nowhere to go. They have to travel to theaters in other cities – and spend their money there instead of here. But I'm convinced that if we had a good, modern theater in this city, it would be extremely popular. What do I mean by a modern theater? Well, I firmly believe that the future is immersive theater.

Immersive theater is where the audience becomes part of the performance. There's no stage – just one shared space for actors and spectators alike. You don't just watch a play – you experience it. Immersive theater works best in a large open area, where groups of audience members can move around to watch different scenes of the play in different parts of the theater. And I think the city's warehouse would make a wonderful immersive theater. But it isn't just about art. Immersive theater is also a great business. The best shows attract rich international tourists who are prepared to pay premium prices. If we turned the warehouse into a theater, it would make a lot of money. This money could be spent on schools, roads and other important things for the city. If you like the sound of that, please support my proposal.

C: Thank you, Violet. Very interesting. Our final finalist is Florian Quirk.

F: Thank you. Let me ask you a question. What … is the purpose … of art? To keep bored people busy? To make money from rich tourists? No, I don't think so. Art is about opening your mind to new experiences, new emotions. It's about losing yourself … and finding yourself. Great art makes you laugh; it makes you cry; it makes you think. It helps you see things you've never seen, feel things you've never felt, understand things you've never understood. In short, the purpose of art … is to give a purpose … to life. That's why I'd like to turn the warehouse into a gallery of modern art. A place where audiences can view the works of today's best artists, including exhibits by some of the talented artists from this city. And if we make it free of charge, all the people of this city can enjoy the exhibits, displays and live performances. So if you really want to use this space for the arts, then forget about business plans and community projects. Let's create a gallery that will change the way the people of this city think … forever. Thank you.

C: OK, thank you. Well, I must say, all three proposals sound excellent! If the city council had three warehouses, maybe we could do all of those wonderful things. But we only have one warehouse, unfortunately, so we need to make a choice. I'd like to call a 15-minute break now so we can …

Lesson 9.2, Listening, Exercise B

9.5 **Z = Zoe J = Jacob**

Z: So, Jacob, how's your creative writing class going?

J: Really well, thanks, Zoe. This week, we've been writing flash fiction. That's where you have to write stories within a word limit, usually 1,000 words. It's really difficult.

Z: Really? Why?

J: Because you have to make every word count. It makes you think hard, and that makes you more creative.

Z: Yes, I see what you mean, but 1,000 sounds very extreme.

J: Well, it isn't as extreme as micro-stories. They're stories on social media sites like Twitter. A whole story told in a 140-character message.

Z: You're joking, right?

J: No, I'm not. Do you want to hear one of my favorites? 'It was him! She sat in embarrassed silence. She wondered if he even knew she existed. He sat beside her, wondering the same. Nobody spoke.'

Z: OK. It isn't much of a story, is it? I mean, nothing happened.

J: No. But it's about creating a powerful scene, and characters with real emotions.

Z: Characters? You just said 'he' and 'she'.

J: Well, it's usually better if the writer provides less information, so that you, the reader, can create the missing information from your own imagination.

Z: Uh, OK.

J: OK, so here's another one. 'Alone, he ran nervously into the dark forest. A shadow. "Who's there?" he shouted. "Don't worry," whispered a cold voice. "You aren't alone."'

Z: Oh, that's better. I see what you mean about using your imagination. I like the twist at the end.

J: What do you mean by 'twist'?

Z: It's when something happens in the story that you didn't expect. I mean, you think he's alone, but then he isn't. It's really powerful, isn't it?!

J: Yeah, I think so. There are also some groups on social media that write collaborative stories: stories that are created by a large group of people working together. So for example, I'll write the beginning of a story, in one 140-character message, and then you'll write the next part of the story, and so on. Eventually, we'll end up with an amazing story.

Z: Ah. It reminds me of a game we played when I was a child. We called it 'Pass the paper'. You write one line of a story on a sheet of paper, fold it down and pass it to the next player, who writes the next line, and so on. We could play it now, if you like. You'll enjoy it!

J: No, thanks. It isn't my kind of thing. But there are actually websites now that do similar things. You write a sentence online, and then someone else writes the next sentence, and so on. I know some people in my class use websites like those to give them ideas. Of course, most of the stories are trash, but it's all about opening your mind to new ideas.

Z: Yes, I'm sure.

J: And there's another one where each person can just write three words. Some of the stories are really funny.

Z: Oh, yes. That reminds me of another game we frequently played when I was a student in California, 'Add a word'. Do you know it? It's when a group of you sit in a circle. The first person says the first word from a sentence, like 'My'. And then the next person says the next word. For example …

J: Favorite?

Z: OK, yes. So, my – favorite, uh, frog.

J: Lives?

Z: Uh, under.

J: My.

Z: Uh, bed?

J: OK. Uh, because.

Z: He.

J: Can't.

Z: Afford.

J: A.

Z: Hotel?

J: Yeah, why not. Hey, that's a great game for collaborative stories, Zoe. You see! When you work together, you come up with ideas that you'd never have if you were on your own.

Z: Sure. So is that how you always come up with new ideas?

J: Not always, no. I sometimes use story dice.

Z: Story dice?

J: Yes. I have a set of 12 dice, and each one has six pictures, one on each side.

Z: OK.

J: So if I'm figuring out an idea for my story, I throw six dice. Then I have to use all six pictures in my story. Let's say the pictures on my dice show a castle, the color blue, an angry face, a bag of money, a motorcycle and a fish. So I have to write my story so that it includes all those things.

Z: Wow! So how about 'My fish was angry because he crashed his expensive motorcycle into a blue castle'?

J: Well, that's very creative, but it has to sound natural and believable. The story can have up to 1,000 words, remember.

Z: Cool. OK, I'm going to try to write it.

J: Great. It won't be easy … but it should be fun!

UNIT 10

Lesson 10.1, Listening, Exercise B

10.2 **R = Robert V = Vicky**

R: Would you mind if I borrowed your laptop for a few minutes?

V: No, of course not. Go ahead. Just bear in mind that it's really slow and it keeps crashing all the time.

R: Sounds like you need a new one.

V: Yeah, I know. I'm trying to buy one, but … it's difficult.

R: What do you mean?

V: Well, I went to the electronics store last week. They had over 100 laptops to choose from. After about three hours in the store, looking at every single laptop, I found two that I liked, but I was of two minds and I couldn't decide which one to buy. It was horrible. In the end, I gave up! But never mind. I still have my old computer, so it isn't so bad.

R: Ah. Sounds like the Paradox of Choice.

V: What's that?

R: Well, the name comes from an American psychologist, Professor Barry Schwartz. According to Professor Schwartz, most people assume that having lots of choices is always a good thing. But he's shown that in fact too many choices is bad for us. It makes us stressed, so we can't make decisions.

V: Uh … OK. So why do stores give us so many choices? Surely they'd sell more if they reduced the number of choices?

R: Exactly. The problem is, most companies still think more is better. But a few smart companies have realized that they'll sell more if they offer fewer choices. I read recently that a shampoo company cut the number of shampoo choices from 26 to 15. Everyone thought they'd lose sales, but in fact, their sales went up by ten percent.

V: Really? Wow! So fewer choices is better.

R: Yes, in general. But of course it's better to have some choice than no choice at all – that's just common sense.

V: Right.

R: So with your laptop, you should have gone to a smaller store. If you'd done that, you'd have had fewer choices, but your decision would have been much easier. The store where I bought mine had just three laptops to choose from. One was too expensive; one was too basic; the third one was absolutely fine, so I bought it. It took me five minutes. And I'm very happy with it.

V: Wow! I could never do that. I'd be worried that I'd missed the chance to buy a better computer somewhere else.

R: That's because you're a perfectionist.

V: A perfectionist? What's that?

R: It's a person who always looks for the perfect thing to buy. You can't relax unless you're sure you've studied every option and chosen the best one. And even after you've made a decision, you still worry that you've made the wrong choice.

V: Yeah, that definitely sounds like me! For example, I went shopping for some new shoes last week. After about six hours, I finally bought a pair. But when I got them home, I regretted my decision immediately. I realized that they weren't perfect and I shouldn't have bought them. So I took them back to the store to get my money back. Then I bought a different pair of shoes, but I took them back to the store a few days later. In the end, I bought the first pair again.

R: Yes, you're definitely a perfectionist. I, on the other hand, am what I call a 'quick decider'.

V: What's that?

R: It's a person who makes quick decisions without worrying about perfection. When I'm shopping for new jeans, for instance, and I find some jeans that are good enough, I buy them and stop worrying about them. And I never take them back to the store – unless they're damaged, of course. Once I've made up my mind, I stick with my decision.

V: Wow! You're so lucky. I could never do that!

R: Well, you think it's impossible, but maybe it's all in the mind. I think you can become a quick decider – you just need to put your mind to it! It'll make life much easier.

V: Yes, you're right. I'll definitely do that! From now on, I'm going to be a quick decider. But, uh, what if I change my mind later?

Lesson 10.2, Listening, Exercise B

10.3 D = David B = Barbara A = Alice L = Leo

D: Hello, and welcome back to *All in the Mind*. On today's show, we're talking about habits. I'm joined by Professor Barbara Janovich, an expert in habits. Welcome to the show, Professor.

B: Thanks, David.

D: So, Barbara, why do we develop bad habits? And why are they so hard to break?

B: Well, the best way to understand habits is to break them into four parts. First, there's a cue, which might be something that you see or hear or feel. So in your example with fast food, the cue might be that you're driving in your car and you see a sign for a fast-food restaurant. Or maybe you're walking through a shopping mall and suddenly you smell the fast food.

D: Oh, yes. That smell always makes me want to eat fast food, even when I'm not hungry! I wish it didn't, but it does!

B: Exactly. So the next stage is the routine – the actions you always take. So this is where you go into the fast food restaurant, order your food and eat it. In a true habit, you can do all of this without really thinking – it kind of happens to you, and your brain almost shuts off.

D: OK.

B: And then the third part is the reward: something nice happens. In this case, the sugar and salt in the food cause your brain to produce feel-good chemicals.

D: OK, so the cycle is cue, routine, reward. But you said there are four parts. What's the fourth part?

B: Well, this is the dangerous part: the craving. Let me explain. If you repeat the cycle a few times, your brain produces those feel-good chemicals earlier and earlier in the process. So instead of being part of the reward, you get that nice feeling at the cue stage – when you see the restaurant sign, for example, or you smell the food and you know the reward is coming soon. And now you have a problem: you've had the good feeling, but you haven't had the reward yet. This creates the craving – a powerful need to get your reward. Now you can't relax until you have your reward.

D: Ah. I wish I'd known about all this a few years ago! But I guess it's too late for me now. Is there anything I can do to break the cycle?

B: Yes, but isn't easy. You can't stop the cues, and you still need the reward. So the trick is to change the routine. So for example, I always keep a package of low-fat salty snacks in my bag. That means that when I drive past a sign for a fast-food restaurant, I treat myself to a snack from the package.

D: Uh, can I try one of those?

B: Sure! Help yourself.

B: So the cue is the same, and the reward is similar – salty food – but I've changed the routine. Of course, salty snacks aren't perfect, but they're a lot cheaper and healthier than a burger and fries.

D: Sounds good. OK, so earlier we asked our listeners to call in to tell us about their bad habits. Our first caller is Leo. Leo, what's your habit?

L: Hello. Well, it's coffee. I drink about eight cups a day, but I don't even like it very much! I wish I could stop, but I can't control myself.

B: OK. Well, let's start with the first cup of coffee each day, Leo. What's your cue for drinking it?

L: It's when I arrive at work. I always make myself a cup of coffee before I check my emails.

B: How long does it take to get to work?

L: About an hour. Why?

B: Well, it sounds like the reward isn't really the coffee, but a five-minute break after your long, tiring trip.

L: Uh, yes, maybe.

B: So now we know the cue and the reward, the question is: is there a different routine that would give you the same reward after your trip to work?

L: I suppose I could get myself a glass of water and go for a quick walk around the office.

B: Sounds good.

D: OK, great. I hope your new routine works for you, Leo. I wish we had time to talk about your other seven cups of coffee, but we need to go to our next caller, Alice. What's your bad habit, Alice?

A: Well, actually, I'd like some help creating a new habit. You see, I wish I could run a marathon next year. I go running from time to time, but I want to get into the habit of running every day. I always set myself goals, but nothing seems to work. I really wish I were better organized.

D: Thanks for that, Alice. Professor?

B: Well, first of all, Alice, don't blame yourself. This is a very common problem. If you want to create a new habit, again you need to think about cues and rewards: what will make you remember to go running at the same time every day? How will you reward yourself for being good? So let's start by creating your cue, Alice. When would be a good time of day to go running?

Notes

Macmillan Education Limited
4 Crinan Street
London N1 9XW

Companies and representatives throughout the world

American Language Hub Level 3B Student's Book ISBN 978-1-380-04725-0
American Language Hub Level 3B Student's Book with Student's App
ISBN 978-1-380-04719-9

Written by Jeremy Day and Gareth Rees.

With thanks to Signature Manuscripts for the Grammar Hub pages.

First published 2020

Designed by emc design ltd
Illustrated by Rasmus Juul represented by Lemonade Illustration Agency, Daniel Limon (Beehive Illustration)
Cover design by Restless
Cover photograph by Peathegee Inc/Getty Images
Picture research by Emily Taylor and Victoria Gaunt
Café Hub videos produced by Creative Listening
Café Hub video scripts written by James and Luke Vyner

The authors and publishers would like to thank the following for permission to reproduce their photographs:

Alamy Stock Photo Samuel Bay p62(tl,tr), Chris Howes/Wild Places Photography p68(cl), Maskot p100(tr), Mladen Mitrinovic pXIX(tr), roibu p98(t), Kurt De Leon Wulf p104(r); **Bridgeman Images** Passengers in the dining room aboard the airship LZ 127 'Graf Zeppelin' during the trip from Germany to America, 1928 (b/w photo)/© SZ Photo/Scherl p116(b); **Corbis** 94-95(background); **DIGITALVISION** pp82(b), 118(background), Uwe Krejci p114(tl); **Eden Full Goh** p86(r); **Getty Images** pp62(bl), 68(bl), 71(background), 97, 112(a), Alija pp100(br), 101, al_irfan78 pXXI(bl), Alexandros Maragos pp105-106(background), AMe Photo p112(c), Arterra/Contributor p80(3), Jose A. Bernat Bacete p86(l), Ezra Bailey pXXVI, Thomas Barwick p112(d), Caspar Benson pXXI(br), Blend Images – KidStock p65, Bloomberg/Contributor p91(b), Warren Bolster 61, 67(r), brunorbs p78(tcr), cristianoalessandro pXXVII(t), Daisy-Daisy p80(1), Peter Dazeley p67(l), Steve Debenport p98(bc), Nick Dolding p64(br), DrAfter123 p88(t), Blasius Erlinger p109, JackF p112(b), Marlene Ford p68(cr), franckreporter p104(l), Alena Gamm/EyeEm p76(c), JGI/Jamie Grill p117, Mike Harrington pXXIV(tl), Hero Images pp 69, 85, XXIV(cl), Hoffmann Photography p100(tl), iStockphoto pp110-111, iStockphoto/97 p113, iStockphoto/LUHUANFENG p79(br), Thinkstock Images/Monkey Business Images Ltd pXVII(br), iStockphoto/pilipphoto p115(tl), iStockphoto Thinkstock Images/photoncatcher pp106(b)-107(b), iStockphoto/Stevo24 p103(bl), iStockphoto/yang5i pXIX(bl), iStockphoto Thinkstock Images/Gary Blakeley pXVI(b), iStockphoto Thinkstock Images/Gabrielle Morehead p83(background), iStockphoto Thinkstock Images/fleurdrz pXVII(bl), iStockphoto Thinkstock Images/kasto80 pXXI(tl), iStockphoto/Thinkstock Images/tolokonov p105, thejokerstrick pp70(background, t), Chaithanya Krishna Photography p74(c), Mads Perch p97, PictureIndia RF/Asia Images Group p114(tr), David Madison p62(br), maxchu pXXIV(tr), Anik Messier p66(r), Dean Mitchel pp98, 99(b), moisseyev p80(2), Kelvin Murray p78(tcl), Richard Newstead pp92-93, PhotoDisc p 63(br), Quiet Noise Creative pXXI(tr), Ingrid Rasmussen/Design Pics p80(4), Lew Robertson pp79(cl),(t) Douglas Sacha p78(bcl), shironosov p66(m), Cultura RM Exclusive/BRETT STEVENS p76(t), Hulton Archive/Stringer 102(tr), SuperStock p68(br), Hindustan Times/ Contributor p74; **Gilaxia** XXVII(b); **Imagesource** pXVII(tl); **Macmillan Education Limited** Paul Bricknell pXVII(tr); **PhotoDisc** pp94(br), 95(cl,b), Getty Images pXIX(br), Getty Images/Anthony Saint James p71(background-Tennis); **REX/ Shutterstock** Oombrella/Bournemouth News p90(r), Bazmark Films/Warner Bros./Kobal p103(br), Flyte/Solent News p90(l); **Science Photo Library** SPUTNIK p116(t); **Shutterstock** Chesky p80(6), Olga Danylenko p66(l), Gorodenkoff p64(bl), SpeedKingz p80(5), thodonal88 p114(tm); **Thinkstock Images** Klaus Vedfelt pXVI(t), vchal p81, vichie81 p100(bc), vladislavnosick p76(b), Westend61 pp62(bl), 73, Ross Woodhal p68(tl), Kathrin Ziegler p89, zodebala p74(b), p75: **Westend61** p115(b); **123RF**/ belchonock pXXVIII, handmadepictures p78(bl), Somchai Jongmeesuk p115(tm), Nadezda Murmakova pXIX(tl), raptorcaptor p78(br).

Commissioned photographs in the Café Hubs by Creative Listening.

Printed and bound in Uruguay
2023
7